FORGOTTEN VIRGINIA

VOLUME II

A CONTINUATION OF DERELICTION AND DECAY IN THE OLD DOMINION

SEAN TOLER

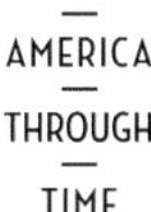

AMERICA
—
THROUGH
—
TIME

Dedicated to those loved ones we have lost along our way,
as well as to those loved ones who we are
fortunate enough to still have in our lives.

AMERICA THROUGH TIME®
An imprint of SUTTON PUBLISHING INC.
www.through-time.com

First published 2025
Copyright © Sean Toler 2025

ISBN 978-1-63499-549-8

All rights reserved. No part of this publication may be reproduced, stored in a retrieval
system or transmitted in any form or by any means, electronic, mechanical, photocopying,
recording or otherwise, without prior permission in writing from Sutton Publishing Inc.

Typeset in Trade Gothic 10pt on 15pt
Printed and bound in England

CONTENTS

INTRODUCTION

Welcome to volume two of *Forgotten Virginia*. I have been working hard since the first volume was published, driving backroads and capturing photos in hopes of being able to put together another book. I have tried to collect as much history about the places in these photos as I could, and while I was not able to gather the histories of all of the places included in the book, I hope that you will be intrigued by that which I was able to discover. In this book you will find more photos, more words, more history, and hopefully more to capture your interest. So, please, sit back and enjoy *Forgotten Virginia Volume II*.

1

BACKROAD WANDERINGS

Time. How many stories have been written or movies filmed dealing with the subject of turning back the clock or finding a way around it altogether? How many times have we looked back on a past event and asked ourselves "What if?" while wishing we could somehow go back in time and change the outcome of that particular event? Unfortunately, that is not a possibility. Once a moment has passed us by, it then becomes history, forever to be inscribed upon the pages of the proverbial annals of time.

The passing of time also brings along with it decay. Whether it be the numerous and various materials, natural or artificial, that can be found upon the earth, or whether it be our own bodies, everything eventually decays. Even a relationship can decay if left unnurtured and neglected. Life has a way of passing us by before we realize just how much time has slipped beyond our grasp.

Take the home in Photo 1 as an example. This old home is not located far from my own. It has sat vacant for more than a decade, although someone does come by periodically to mow the grass. Over the years, I have watched it slowly decay. I can easily remember when this house was lived in, and it does not seem as if it were that long ago. However, when scrolling through the timeline of street view photos taken of this house on Google Maps, it seems to have been last lived in sometime around 2012. Even the driveway has now disappeared beneath the grass from lack of use. Time has sped by so quickly that I almost expect to still see a car in the now nonexistent driveway whenever I pass by.

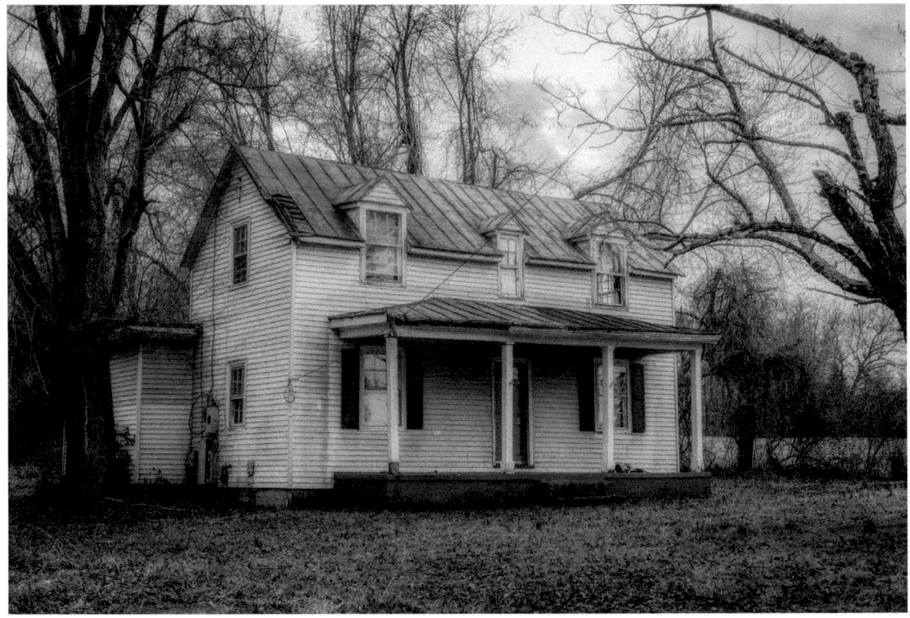

Photo 1: THE MOUNTAIN HOUSE: This home sits not very far down the road from my own and has sat empty for more than a decade.

A few years back, as I was just in the beginning stages of formulating ideas for this second volume of *Forgotten Virginia*, I wanted to begin by telling a few stories of my paternal grandfather, who was, at the time, living in an assisted living facility for military veterans. I had hoped to be able to have this book completed for him to be able to read. Unfortunately, that would not come to fruition as he passed away at ninety-five years of age in 2022. It is never easy to lose a loved one, and as difficult as it was to lose him, there was comfort in knowing that he had lived a long and wonderful life and had made our family's lives better because of it. Fourteen months later, as the sting of his passing was beginning to ease, my dear mother passed away suddenly and unexpectedly at seventy years old. Her death sent shockwaves through my family that are still reverberating even until this day. We had just spoken with her on the phone three days earlier and she was as vibrant and spirited as ever. Just like that, in what seemed like an instant, that vibrance and spirit were now memories. In the months that followed, we all did our best to navigate a life without my mother in it. As we struggled through that navigation, just shy of ten months following the death of my mother, one of my two younger sisters, just as suddenly and unexpectedly as did my mother, passed away as well at the age of forty-four. She died one day before the two-year anniversary of the death of my grandfather. Never in a million years would we, as a family, have even entertained the thought that we would be laying three close family members to rest within a span of two years. Fortunately for my own sake, my relationship with all three of them was close and we all knew that we loved each other very much.

I have not shared this with you to depress you, though that may be an unintended consequence. I have shared this with you to impress upon all of our minds the fragility of life, the elusiveness of time, and the haste by which decay can overtake that which was once pristine when neglect begins to creep in.

As I discussed in the first volume, my paternal grandfather grew up on the family farm in the small town of Oilville in Goochland County. On what appears to have been a warm spring day in 1933, my grandfather and his older sister (he being six years old and she being nine) were playing near the farm on the little bridge that spanned Horsepen Creek at the time. As they were playing, a photographer by the name of William Edwin Booth was traveling by and stopped and asked them if he could take a photograph of them. For the photo, he had my great-aunt sit on the top railing at the edge of the bridge while my grandfather stood directly in front of her, looking up at her and handing her a small bouquet of flowers, while propping his left foot up on the bottom rung of the railing. The photographer titled the photo *The Road to Oilville*. My father was fortunate enough to find the photo in the archives of the Virginia Historical Society, enabling us to still have a copy of it nearly a century after it was photographed. In early 2020, before the world was locked down for the pandemic, I recreated this photograph with my oldest son and my daughter who happened to be around the same ages at the time that my grandfather and his sister were when the original photo was taken. My grandfather had been living at the assisted living facility for a year and a half when the lockdowns took place. Unfortunately, it was several months before I could present him with the framed copy of the original photo alongside the recreated photo of my two children. He loved that gift and kept it on display in his room up until the day he passed away two years later.

At around the same time that I took the recreated photo, I asked my father to take me to where that old bridge had once been located. Upon arrival it was easy to see that the walk to it would not necessarily be smooth as it was surrounded by nearly ninety years of tree growth. After a little bit of a struggle, including my father losing his footing on a hill and tumbling down it (he was fortunately unharmed), we found the site where the bridge once stood. As can be seen in Photo 2, the wooden parts of the bridge have long since rotted away, leaving only the concrete supports on either side of the creek. In the bridge's heyday, Three Chopt Road (the main road between Richmond and Charlottesville at the time) passed over it, along with many travelers while journeying between the two towns.

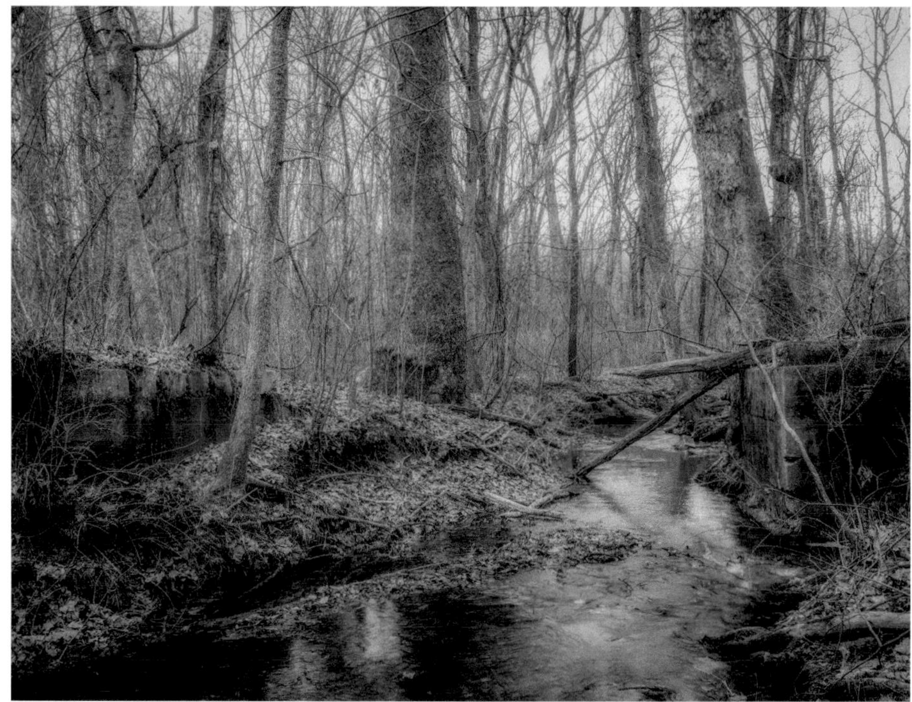

Photo 2: THE OLD OILVILLE BRIDGE: The remnants of what was once the bridge on which my grandfather and his sister posed for a photographer back in 1933.

Not far from the bridge supports are the remains of an old grist mill. My father told me that when he was young, he used to play in the remains whenever his parents would bring him up to the old family farm to visit. This mill was once used to grind grains into flour. Now it sits in ruin, a mere shadow of what it once was. Photos 3 and 4 show how it looked on that cold January day when we visited it.

As we were standing there photographing the mill, I happened to notice the peak of a roof rising above the top of the hill that was next to us. So, my son (who was six at the time) and I decided to venture up the hill to see what we could find (my dad decided to wait for us at the mill until we returned). Upon arriving at the crest, we discovered two old barns and an old Ford pickup there among the trees. Trees which almost surely did not exist in the days when the barns and the truck were used on a daily basis. One can almost imagine these two barns, pictured in Photos 5 and 6, surrounded by green pastures once upon a time.

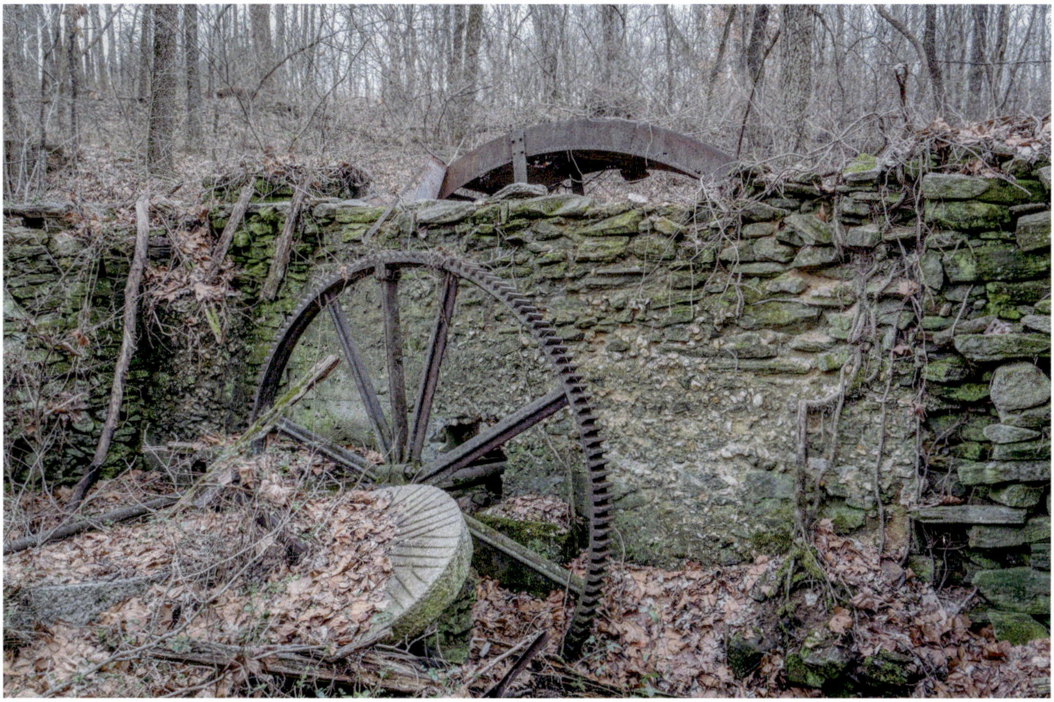

Photo 3: THE MILLER'S LAMENT: This is all that remains of the old grist mill that was located near the farm where my great-great-grandparents had and raised nineteen children; the farm on which my grandfather grew up.

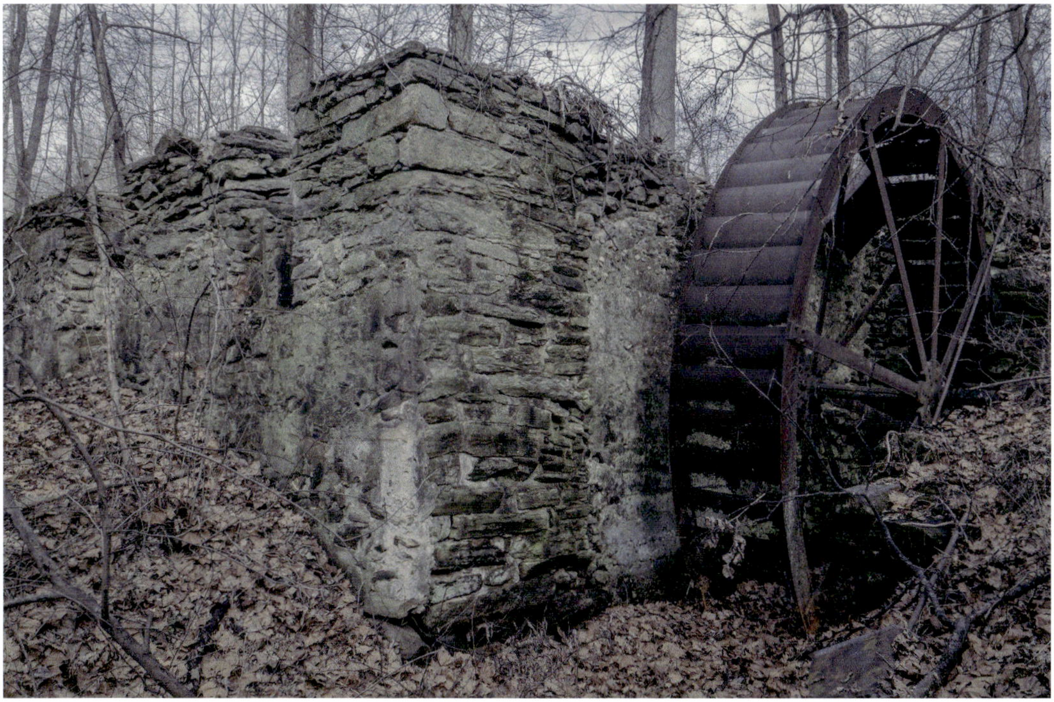

Photo 4: SPIN THE BIG WHEEL: A shot of the back side of the grist mill showing the old water wheel that used to turn the grinder in the mill.

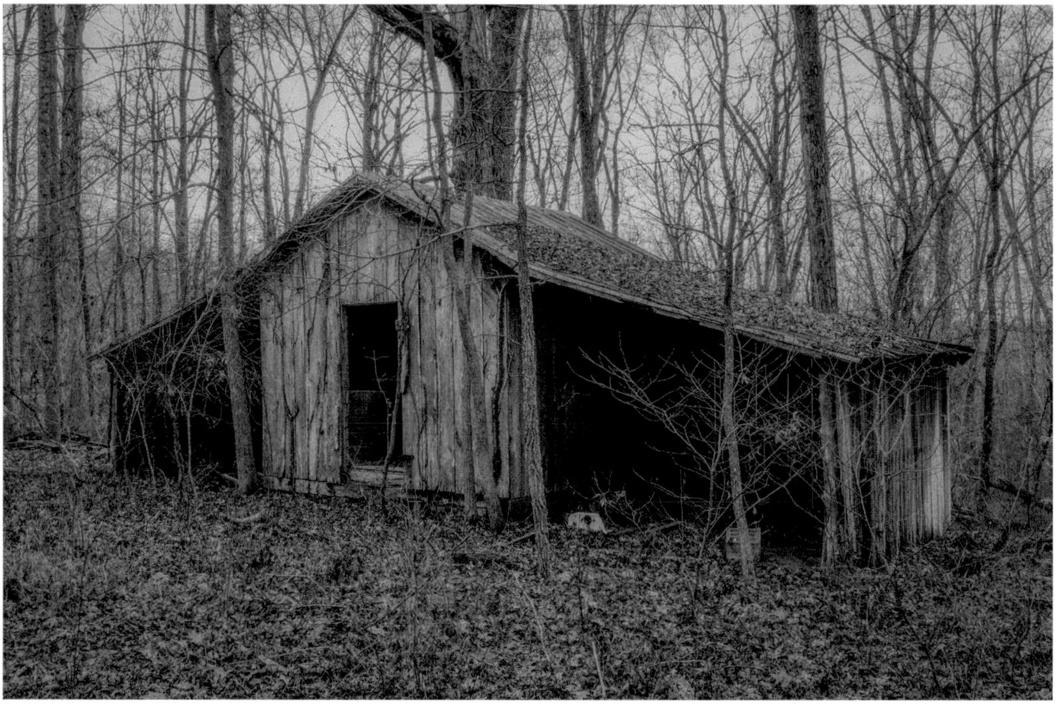

Photo 5: THE OLD HIDDEN BARN: Now surrounded by trees, I can imagine this old barn was once surrounded by rolling hills of green pasture.

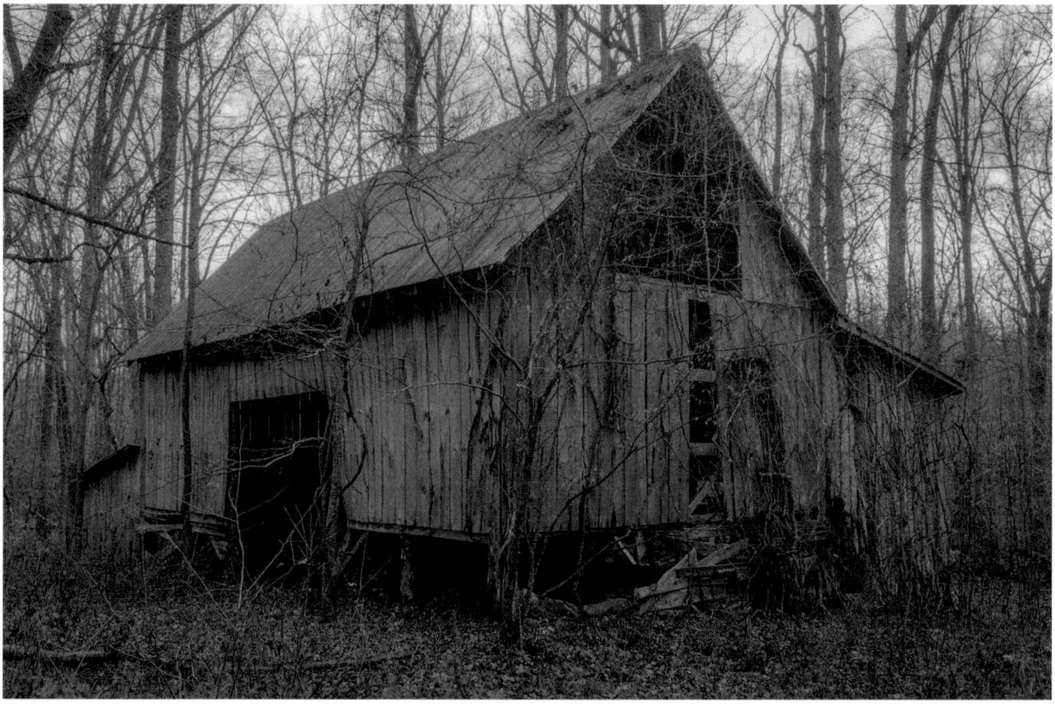

Photo 6: BARN FIND: The second of the two barns that my oldest son and I discovered on the day that we came to see and photograph the old bridge.

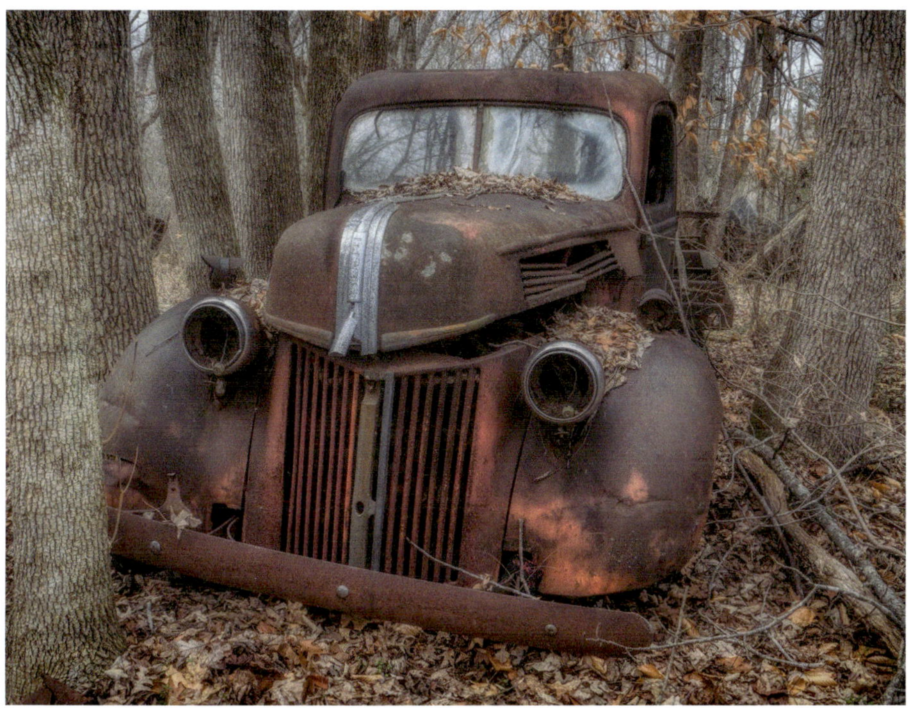

Photo 7: Lost in the Woods: An old pickup truck near the two barns that someone, at some time, parked in that spot and never drove again.

The old pickup, pictured in Photo 7, was last driven many years ago. One can only assume that when it was parked in that location, that none of the trees that have grown up around it would have existed either.

Once we were finished at that location, we got back in the car and my dad had me drive a little way up the road to show me one more house. This house was about 50 yards back in the woods and even with the leaves having fallen from the trees, it was still difficult to see from the road. He told me that this little home was built by his paternal grandfather for a gentleman who had hired him to build it for him. As can be seen in Photos 8 and 9, this was a small home with two rooms. However, it did look as if, at one time, there had been another room attached to the back of the house, perhaps a kitchen.

On an overcast day several weeks later, I left work and went for a drive to see what I could find to photograph. As I was driving, I came to the building shown in Photo 10. This building sits on the side of a busy road. I have seen various people saying different things about what this building once was. Some have said that it was once a truck stop in the days before the adjacent interstate was built. Others have said that it was once a restaurant, while some have even said that there was a bordello on the second floor.

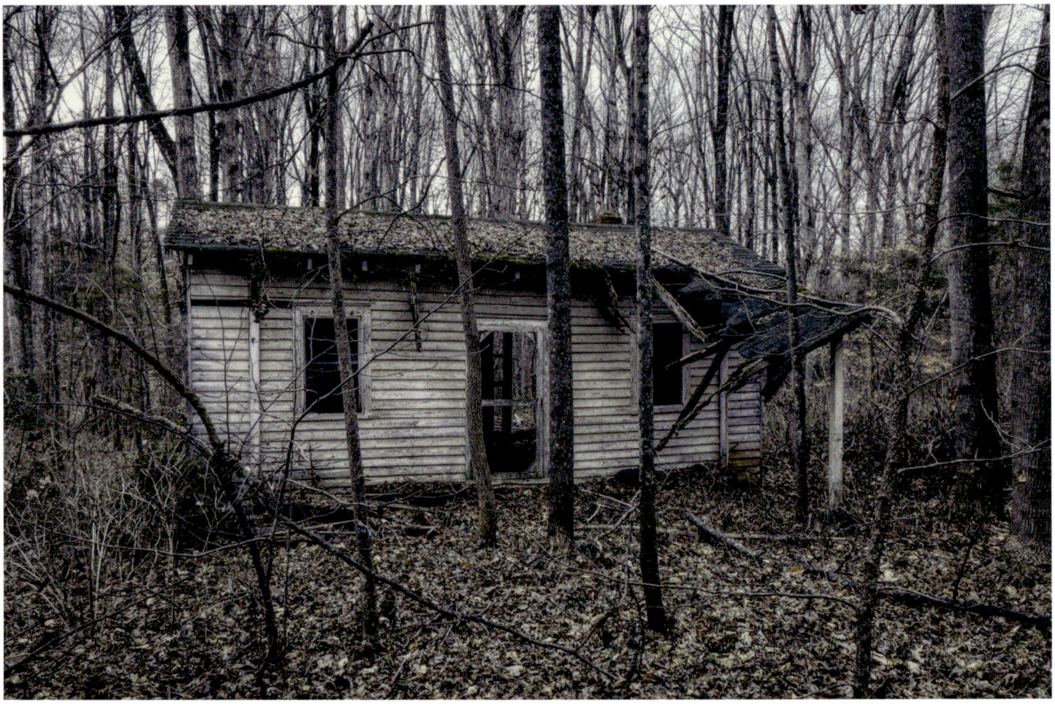

Photo 8: Hidden Amongst the Trees: This small home, which is unknowingly driven past hundreds of times daily, was built by my paternal great-grandfather for a gentleman who hired him to do so.

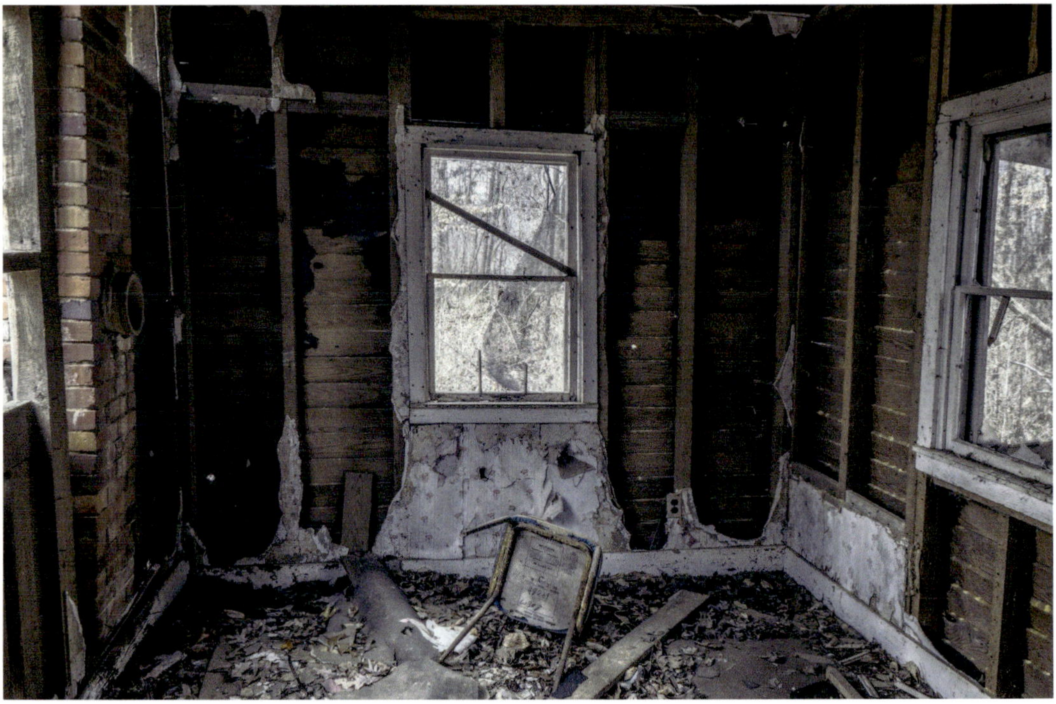

Photo 9: The Old Room: What I imagine was the living area of the tiny home in Photo 8. There was another room to my back when I took this photo that I feel was the bedroom.

I continued on, soon finding some backroads to explore. As I wandered them, I came upon the old farmhouse that is shown in Photo 11. I do not know anything about this home, but to me, it looks like the type of home where family members gathered around the kitchen table to enjoy a home-cooked meal and grandchildren came to excitedly visit their grandparents.

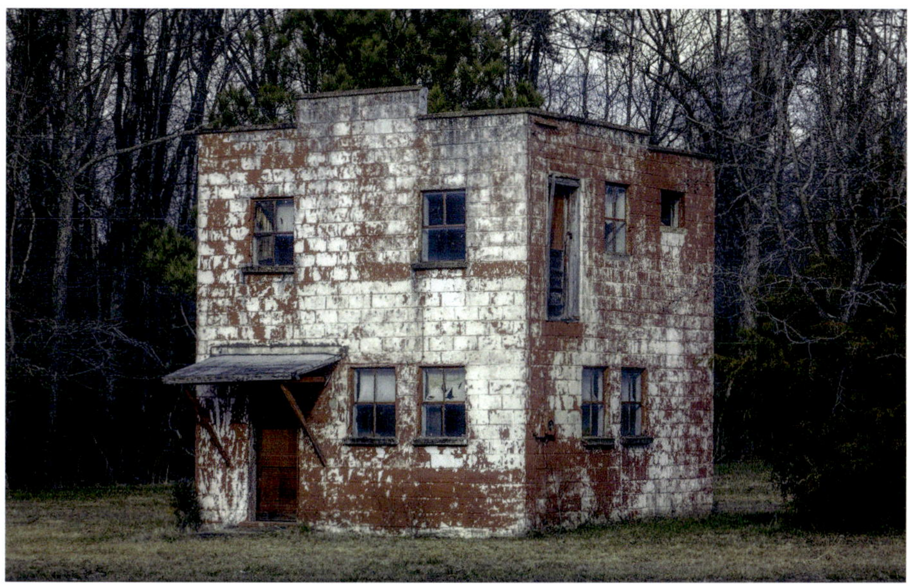

Photo 10: ROADSIDE PIT STOP: In the days before interstates, tiny buildings like this served as truck stops.

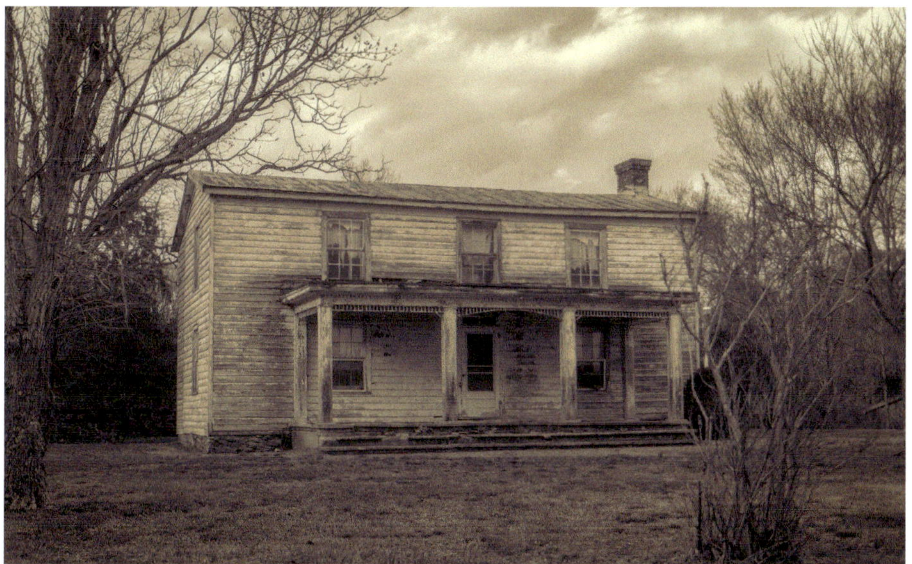

Photo 11: GRANDPA'S FARMHOUSE: This is not really my grandfather's farmhouse; it just looks like how I imagine a farmhouse would look to children in years past as they arrived to visit their grandparents.

The first time I saw someone on social media share a photo of the home pictured in Photo 12, I was instantly intrigued by the fact that the roof was gone, but the bushes that once framed the sides of the front path, that at one time led to the door, were still alive and thriving as if they awaited their long-deceased owner to once again traverse the concourse between them. I decided to drive over one day to see and photograph what was left of this beautiful home. This was the home on Belle Farm in Hanover County. The farmhouse once sat on 335 acres of land. Legend has it that General Robert E. Lee once stopped here, had dinner with the family and stayed the night in this house.

In April 2020, while we were all in the middle of the world being locked down due to the COVID pandemic, my wife and I decided to take our kids on a nice day-long drive through the countryside. Of course, I could not let the opportunity to photograph abandoned buildings along our route pass me by! As we drove along, we came to the house shown in Photos 13 and 14. Apparently, this little house was the home of the person who would serve as the switchman along the stretch of railroad tracks just behind the house. Before there was such a thing as an automatic switch, the switches would have to be manually repositioned. In a lot of cases, a little house was built around the switch itself. This is one of those houses.

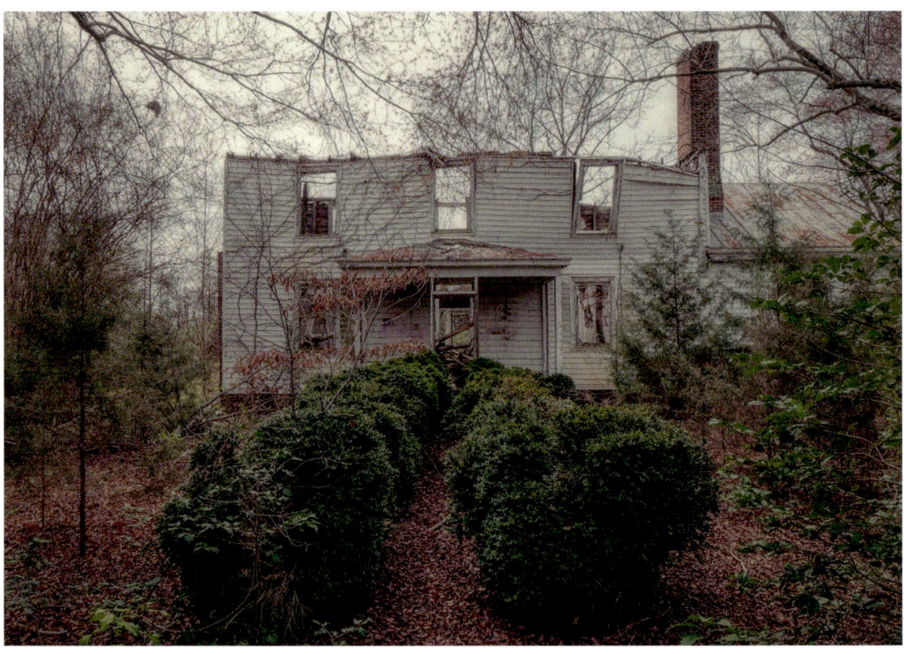

Photo 12: THE PATHWAY BACK HOME: The old home on the former Belle Farm. This home no longer stands, having been demolished for the construction of a warehouse.

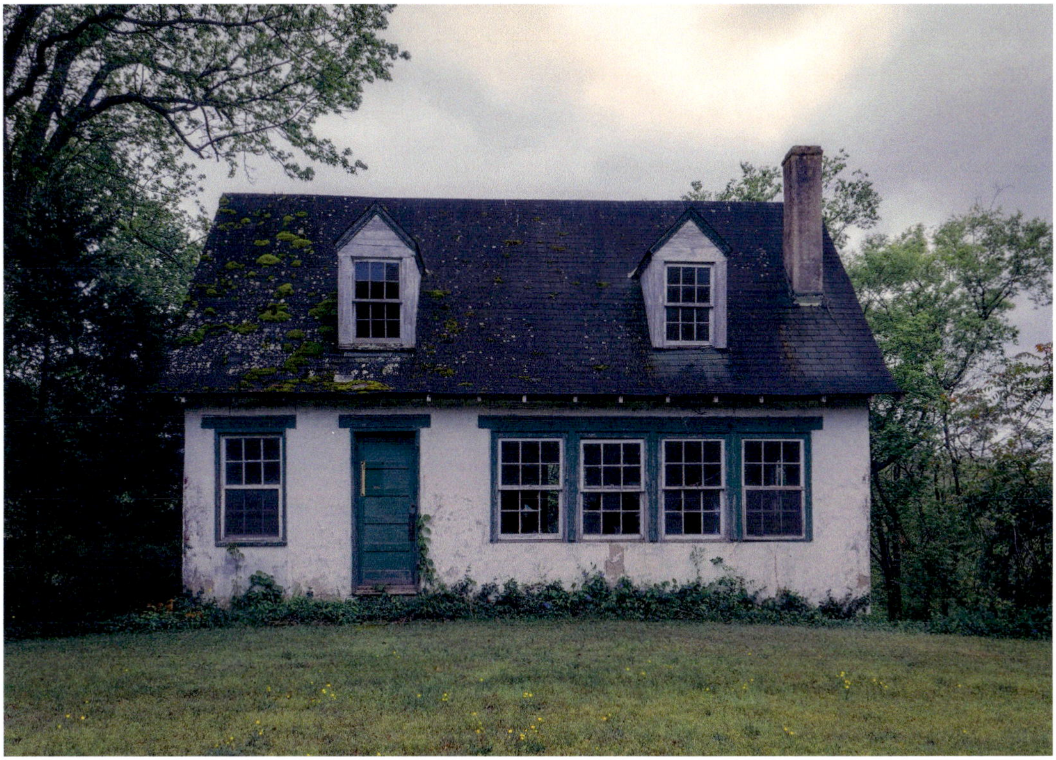

Photo 13: THE FORGOTTEN COTTAGE: Sitting on a grassy knoll overlooking a busy road, this small cottage seems to have been forgotten (although the lawn still seems as though it is maintained).

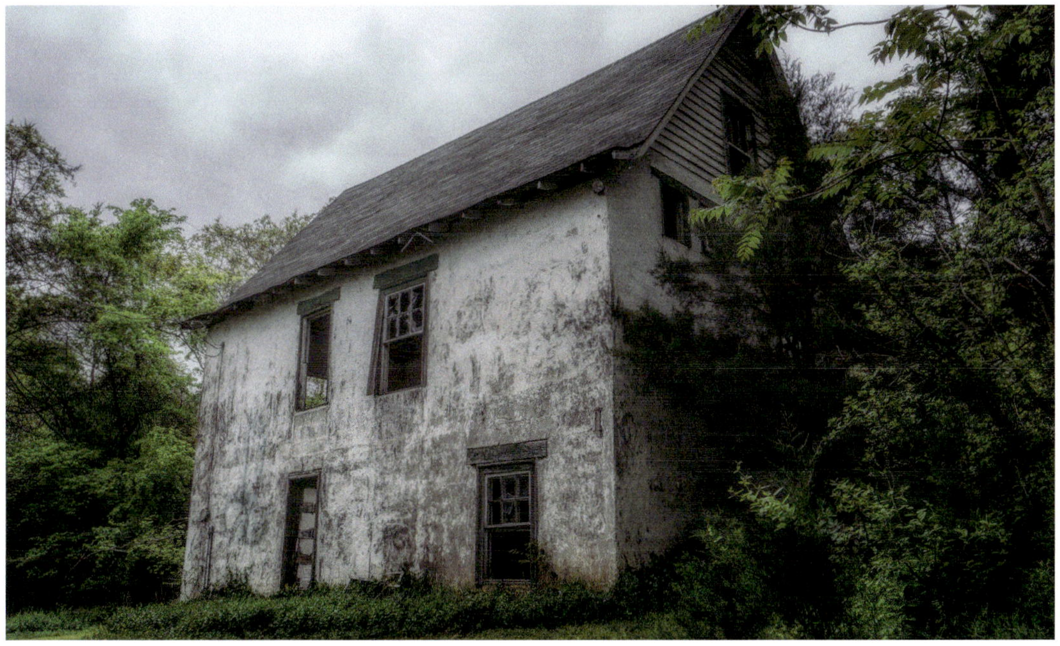

Photo 14: THE BACK OF THE COTTAGE: The back side of the house in Photo 13.

As we continued on our journey, we rode through the little town of Columbia. In its prime, Columbia served as a shipping point for the tobacco trade in Virginia. However, with the dissolution of passenger rail service to the town in the 1950s, it began a long state of decline leading to many of the homes and buildings in the town becoming abandoned. Matters worsened with the flooding caused by Hurricanes Camile and Agnes in 1969 and 1972 respectively. The building shown in Photo 15 sits on the main street through town. It was obviously a business of some sort but has long since served that purpose. The old home shown in Photo 16 sits on a side road.

Not long after leaving the town of Columbia, we arrived at the old Fork Union Train Depot (shown in Photo 17). Built in the early 1900s, this building served as a train depot until it closed in 1970. An old caboose sits next to it (Photo 18). While we were there, we used the opportunity to take some birthday portraits of our youngest son who had just turned three at the time.

Photos 19–22 were taken as we continued our drive that day.

The final photo taken on that day is a building of which I actually had a photo in my first book. However, I had always wanted to get another shot of it on an overcast day, and since we were going to be driving right by it, we stopped to get the shot in Photo 23. This old store sits almost in the geographic center of Virginia. The only problem on this day was that the overcast skies had opened up and it was raining quite steadily. I decided that I would attempt a handheld shot with my right hand, while holding an umbrella in my left. This was more easily dreamed up than actually accomplished as every time I would raise the camera to take the shot, my left thumb would accidentally push the collapse button on the umbrella causing me to frantically get the umbrella reopened so that my camera did not get too wet. This scene was repeated four times until I was finally able to hold the umbrella so that no single part of my hand could touch that button. By the time I had gotten the shot, I felt like I had just lived through a scene in a comedy! If you look closely, you can see the rain in the photo.

Photo 24 almost looks like an old schoolhouse to me. That is what I thought it was when I drove to its location to photograph it back in 2020. This building stood out like a sore thumb as it was located on a cul-de-sac in a subdivision, surrounded by million-dollar homes. As I was photographing it, I asked a gentleman who was out for a walk if he knew its history. He informed me that it was once a barn on the plantation that was once located on that land. In fact, the original plantation house is still standing across the street and has been restored.

Photo 15: ENTERPRISING MISFORTUNES: A former business sits unoccupied now along the main road that passes through the town of Columbia.

Photo 16: THE STILT HOUSE: The building codes when this house was built must have been just a little laxer than they are today! That being said, the stilts do still seem to be holding up the house.

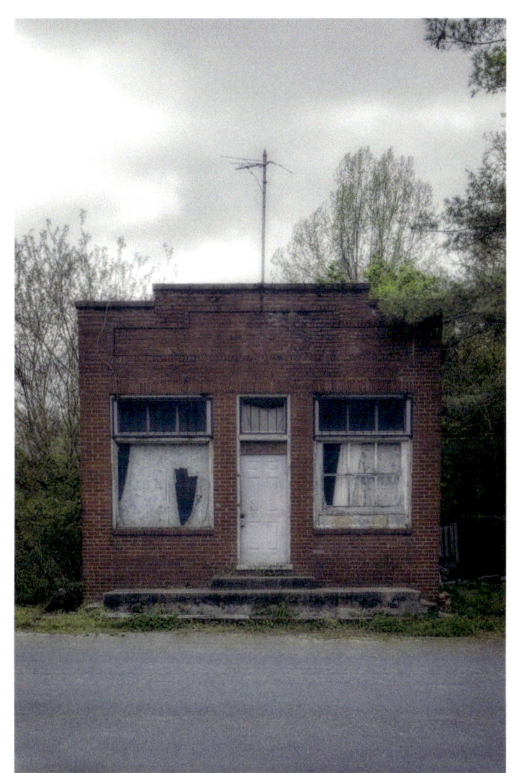

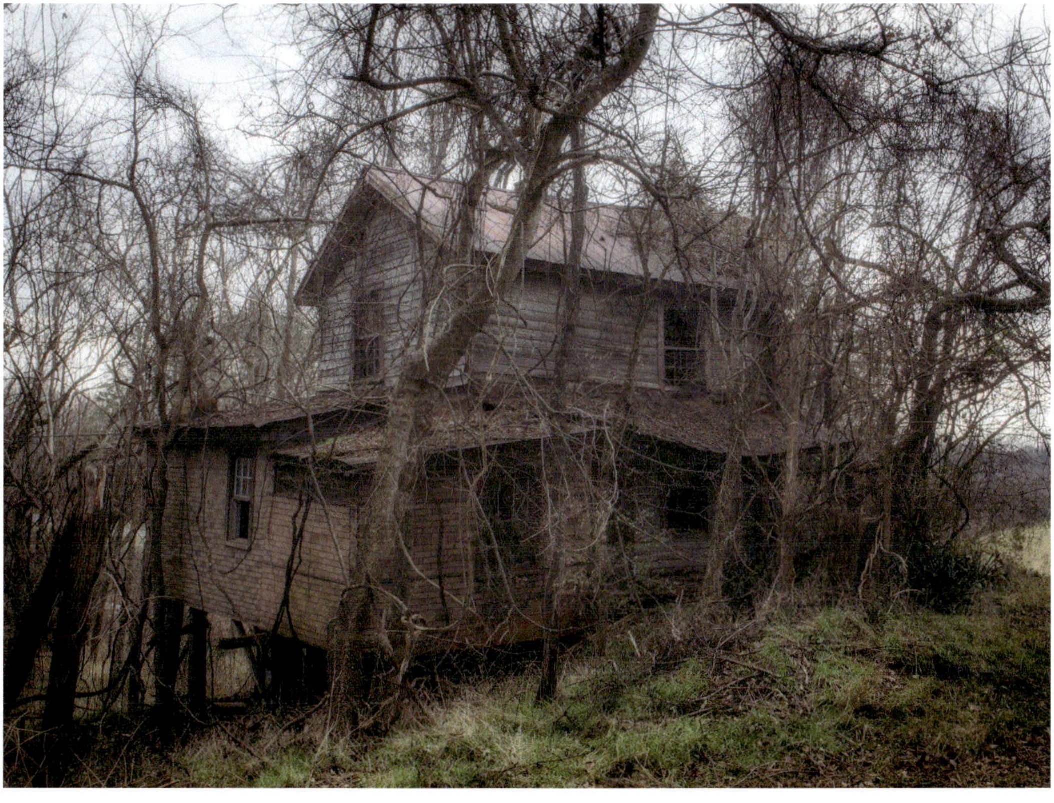

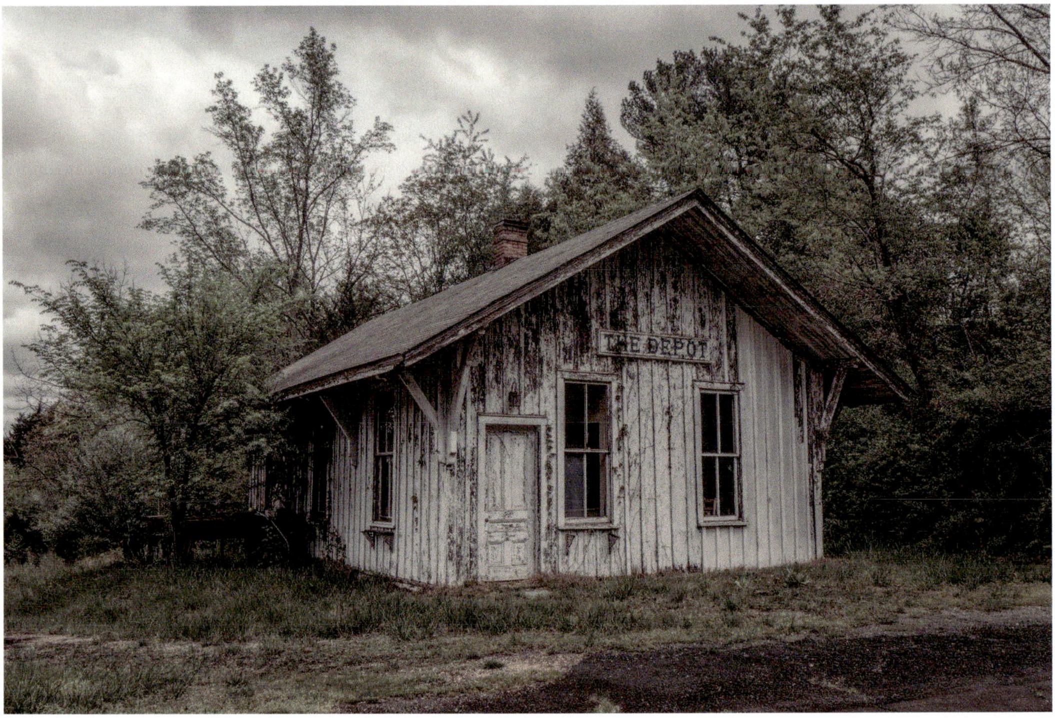

Photo 17: THE DEPOT: The former Fork Union Train Depot.

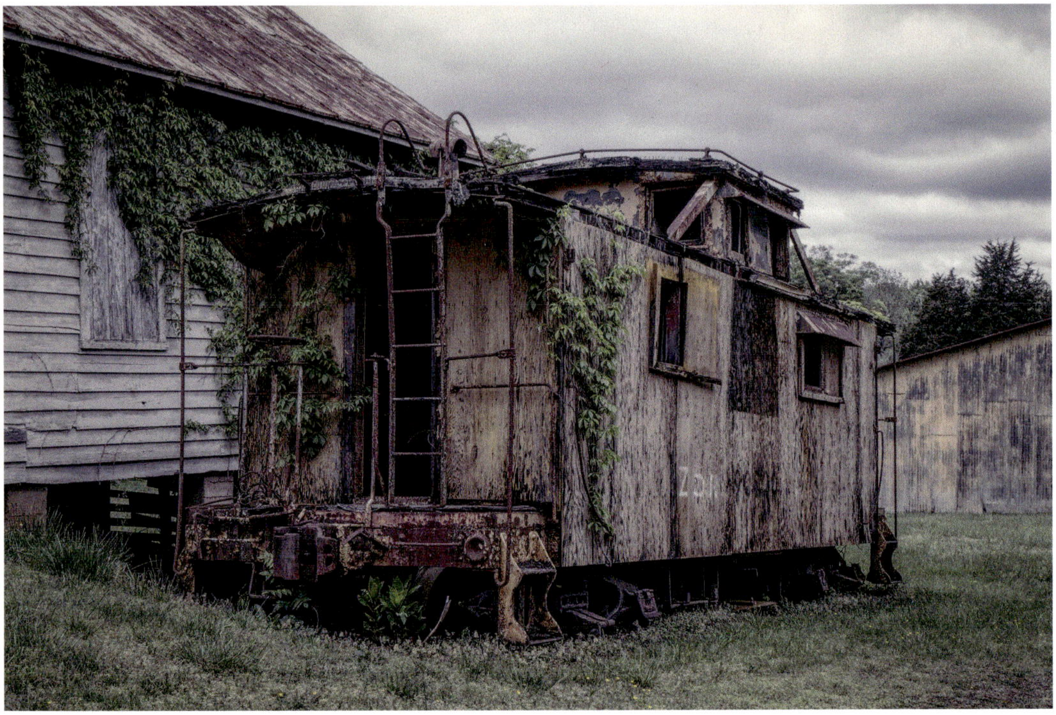

Photo 18: THE OLD TRAIN CAR: Sitting adjacent to the depot in Photo 17, this old caboose is quite the sight to see while driving by.

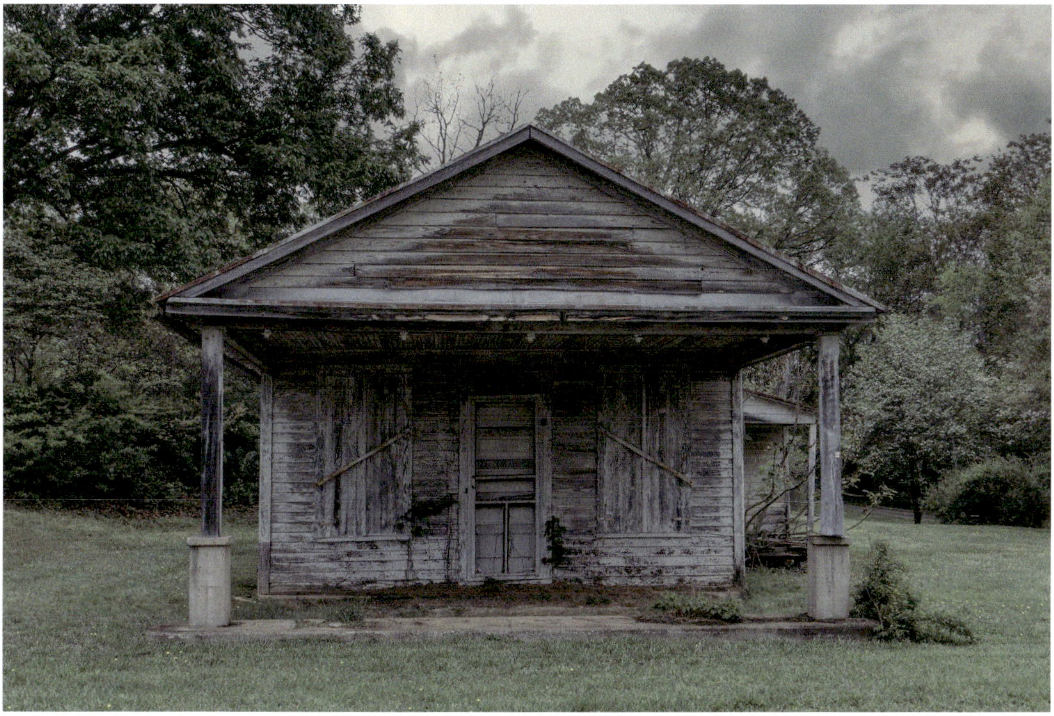

Photo 19: THE OLD STOREFRONT: This old store is not far down the road from the old depot.

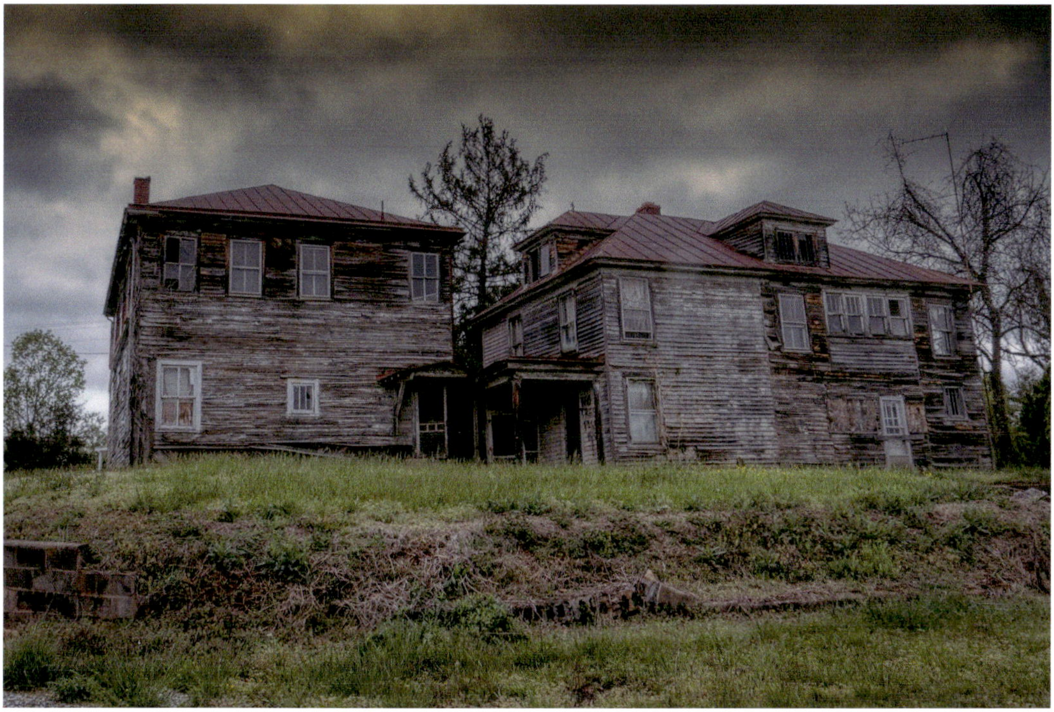

Photo 20: THE OLD NEIGHBORHOOD: A familiar sight to those who frequent Route 29. These buildings look as though someone, at one time, built a connecting covered walkway between them.

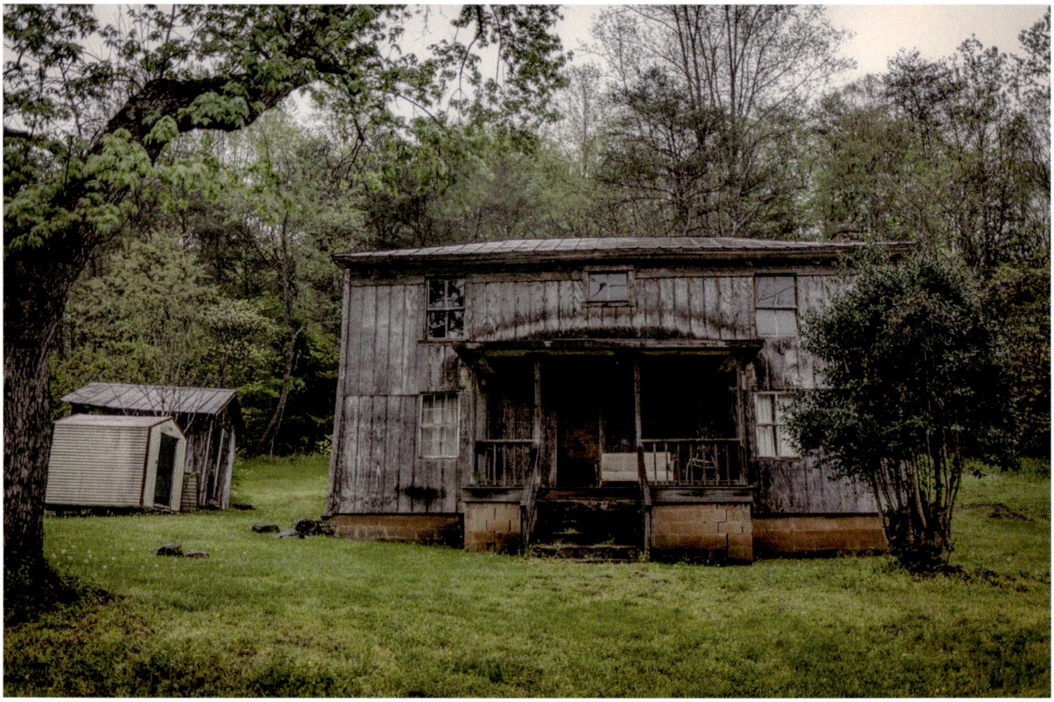

Photo 21: THE GRAY HOUSE: The gray siding on this old home gives it a very ominous look. I wonder how many trick-or-treaters passed by this home over the years without stopping.

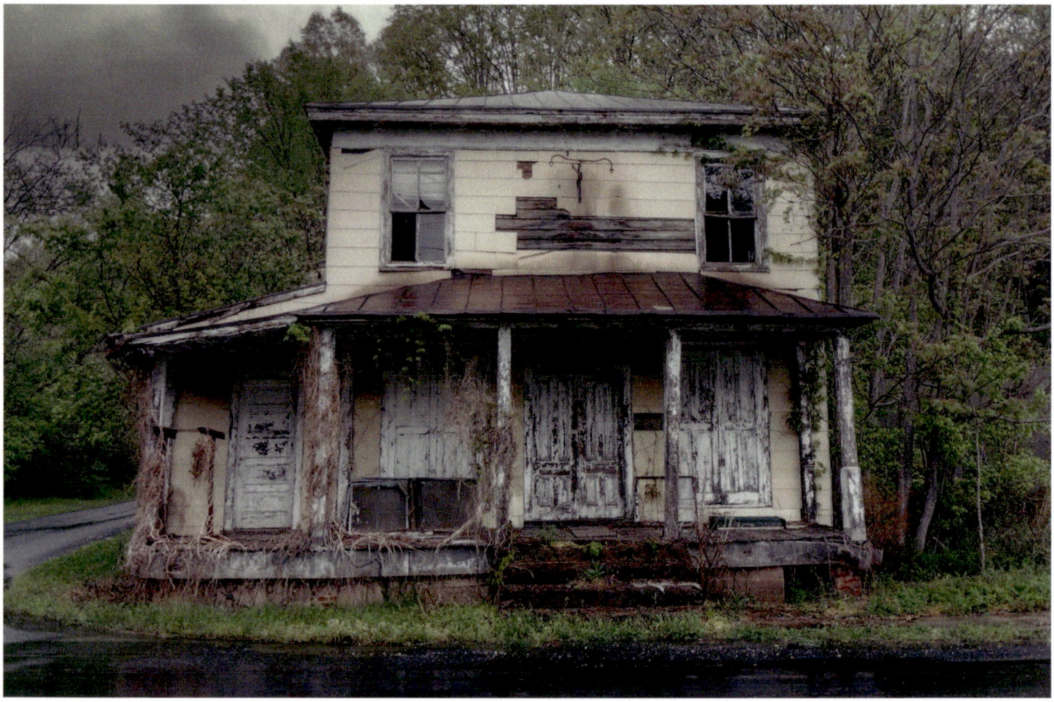

Photo 22: SOLITUDE AND EMPTINESS: As soon as I saw this house, I immediately stopped the car and let down the window to capture it on camera. It was raining quite moderately at the time, but I managed to only get a little wet!

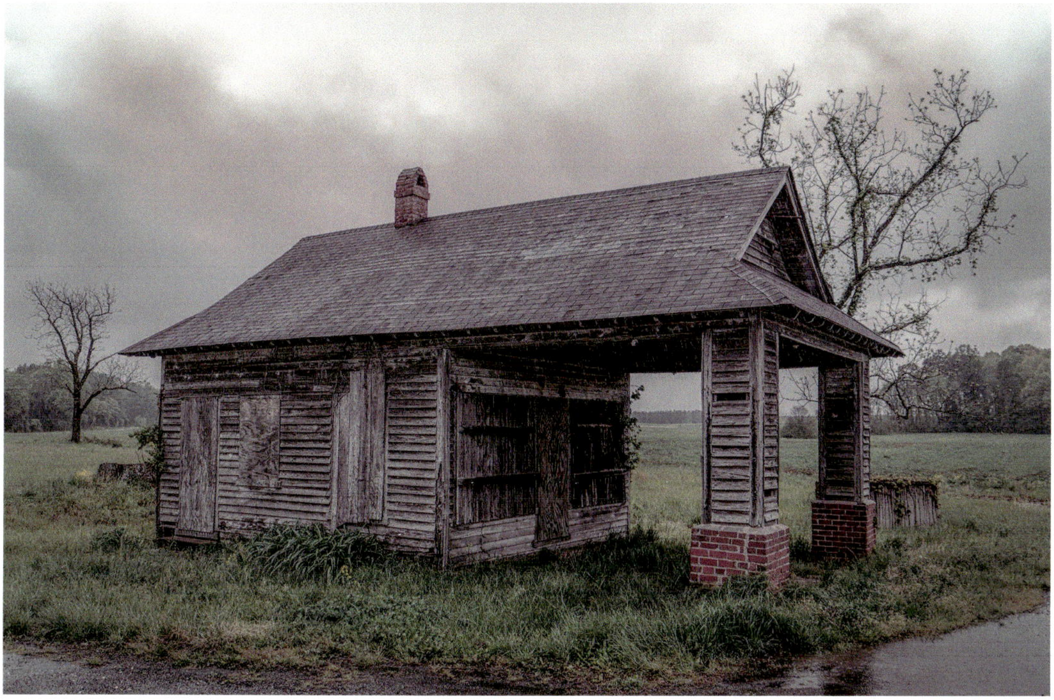

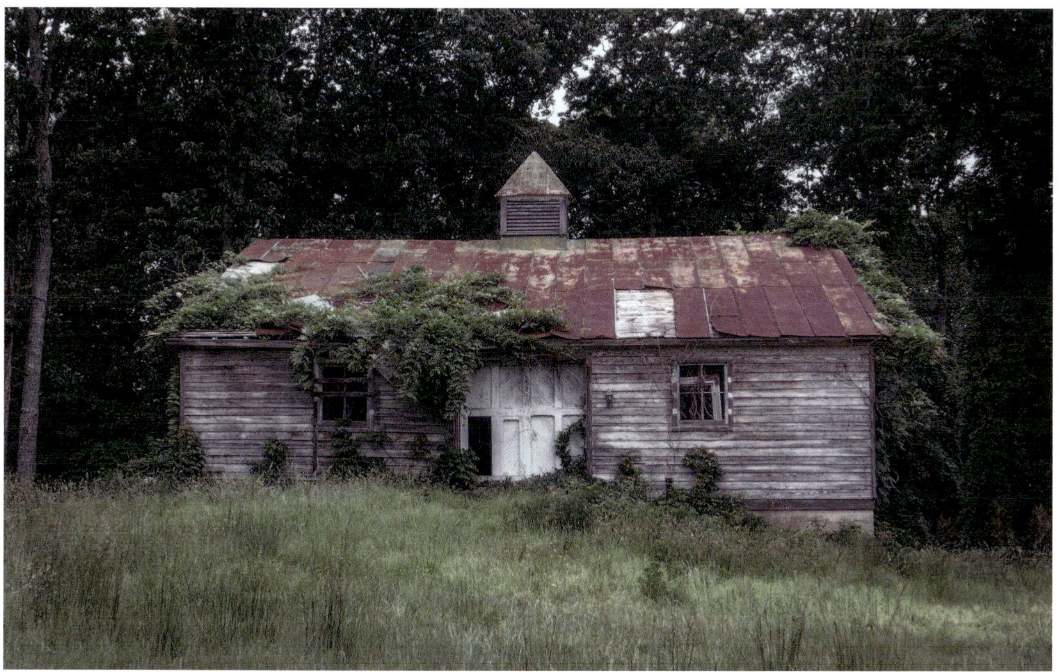

Photo 23: Rainy Day Stop: I imagine that, at one time, there were many stops made at this little store on both pleasant and rainy days.

Photo 24: School Delay: I gave this photo that name because this old barn looks like it could have been an old school to me. This is a case where I am glad that I photographed this building when I did because it has since been demolished.

Later in November of that year, I captured Photo 25. I first discovered this old house as I drove by on the interstate and saw that all of the trees surrounding it had been cleared away, which exposed the once hidden home. I realized that I had a very short window to get over there and photograph it because it would soon meet its demise thanks to the cold steel of a bulldozer. So, I ventured out one day to a predetermined location that would allow me to park and walk through the woods to the house. A rudimentary path had already been cleared that led to the house, so I followed it hoping that I would not be confronted by a construction worker asking why I was there. As I drew near to the house, I saw something out of the corner of my eye. To my left there was a pup tent set up in the woods. It looked like it had been there for quite some time. Just next to it was a crude clothesline with a jacket hanging on it. On the other side of the tent was an old lawn chair. I assumed that a homeless person had been living or still lived there, so I was extra stealthy as I approached and then departed from the house.

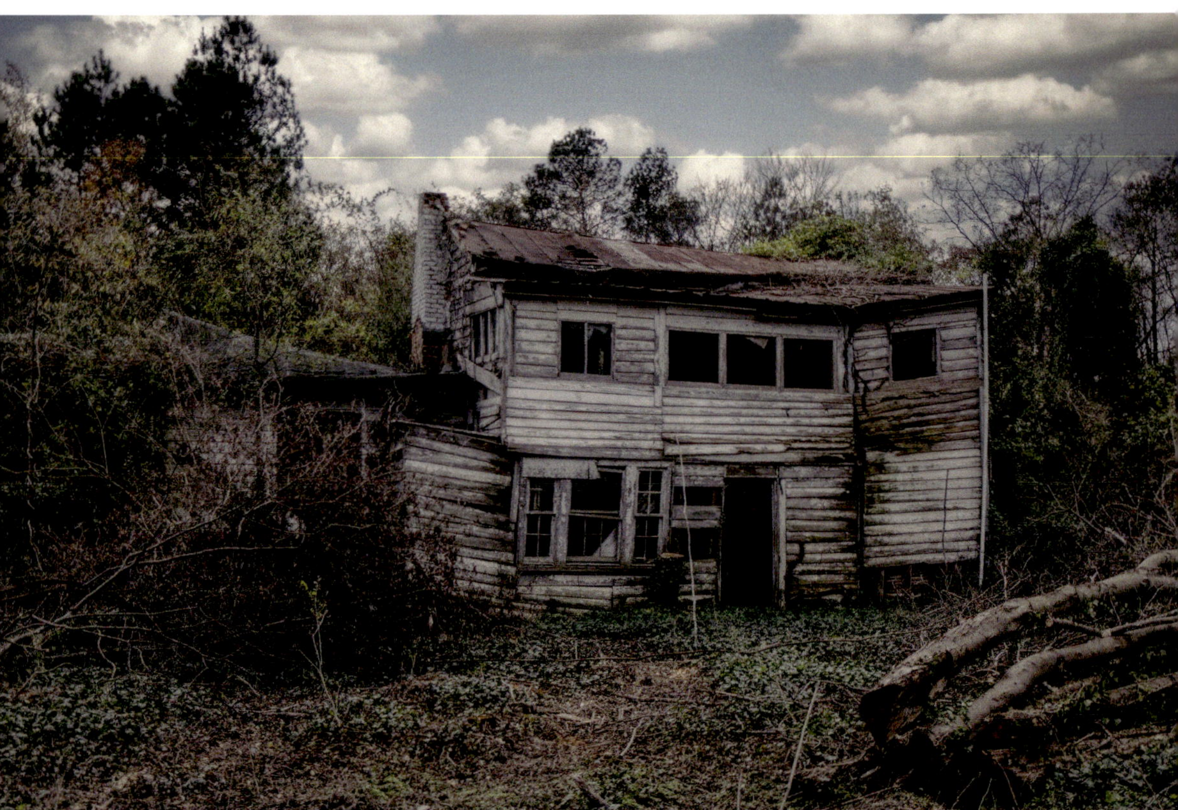

Photo 25: HIDDEN NO MORE: In yet another case where I am glad that I made the effort to photograph an abandoned building quickly, this old home no longer stands. In its place is a fresh crop of town homes.

A month later, in early December, I took my oldest son with me one Saturday to go find and photograph a number of buildings that I had marked on Google Maps. He always likes to go with me because he "doesn't want me to be lonely on those drives." Photos 26, 27, and 28 were our first three stops of the day.

The building pictured in Photos 29 and 30 is an interesting one. I wish I knew some details about it. It definitely looks to me like it was an old school at one time.

I was given permission to take Photos 31–35 by the kind lady who owned the property on where these were located. She told me that the building that is shown in Photos 31 and 32 used to be the home of her grandparents when she was a little girl. Prior to that she told me that it had been a tavern.

The building shown in Photo 36 was our final stop of the day. It was once known as the 250 Trading Post having been named for the route number of the road on which it sat. It looks as though it sustained fire damage at some point.

A couple of weeks later, just a few days after Christmas, my oldest son and I hit the road again with one goal in mind: to get a photo of the bridge pictured in Photo 37. This bridge once spanned the James River at the town of Cartersville. As mentioned earlier, in June 1972 the remnants of Hurricane Agnes caused major flooding in the state. One result of this flooding was the destruction of the center portion of this bridge which was washed away. Today the two sections of the bridge that are connected to land still remain. The portion shown in the photo is on the south side of the river and was originally built in 1884.

After photographing the bridge, my son and I visited one other location. Photos 38 and 39 are of Flannagan's Mill, otherwise known as Trice's Mill. It is said that this mill may have been originally built as early as the 1720s. It is also another location where General Robert. E. Lee stayed the night. An historical marker nearby states "Lee's stopping place. Here at Flannagan's (Trice's) Mill, Robert E. Lee spent the night of April 13–14, 1865, on his journey from Appomattox to Richmond." While it was in use, the mill was used as a water grist mill.

One cold January day in 2021, I noticed that the clouds seemed to have colorful streaks running through them as the sun was setting. I decided to take the opportunity to photograph a nearby building that I had been meaning to photograph. At one time, the building in Photo 40 was the Speed & Briscoe truck stop before the nearby interstate was built. The truck stop has since moved to an exit just off of the interstate. I can personally remember this building serving as the office of a trucking company in the years that I worked just a couple of miles down the road.

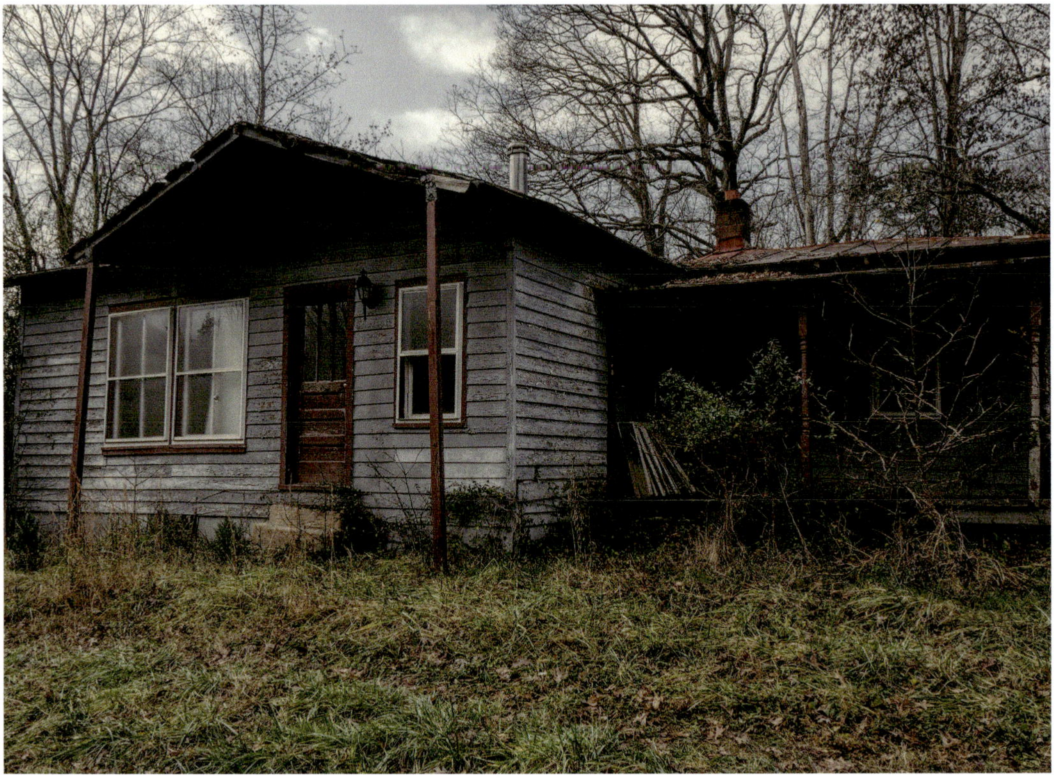

Photo 26: Oᴌᴅ Bᴌᴜᴇ: There is nothing extraordinary about this old home to me. It is not even all that decrepit when compared to a lot of the other buildings I have photographed. What makes it special to me is that my son was with me when I photographed it.

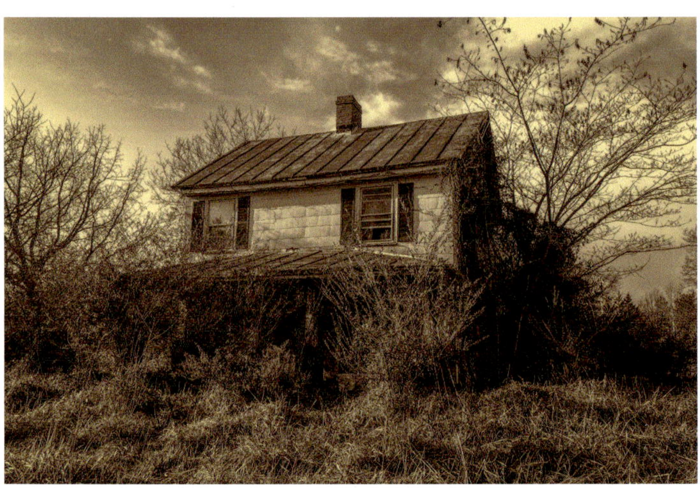

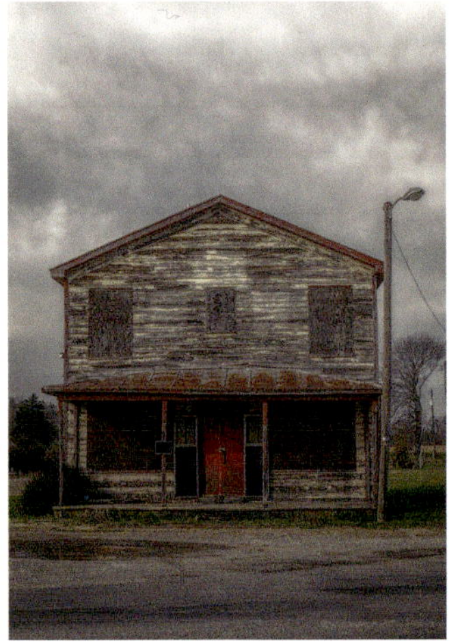

Above left: Photo 27: Oᴠᴇʀɢʀᴏᴡɴ Rᴇᴄᴌᴀᴍᴀᴛɪᴏɴ: An old country home that is slowly being reclaimed by nature. It is kind of neat to look at the different years that this house was photographed in Google Street View to see the reclamation progress.

Above right: Photo 28: Bᴜɪʟᴅɪɴɢ ᴡɪᴛʜ ᴛʜᴇ Rᴇᴅ Dᴏᴏʀ: What I assume was an old store located just down the road from the building in Photos 29 and 30.

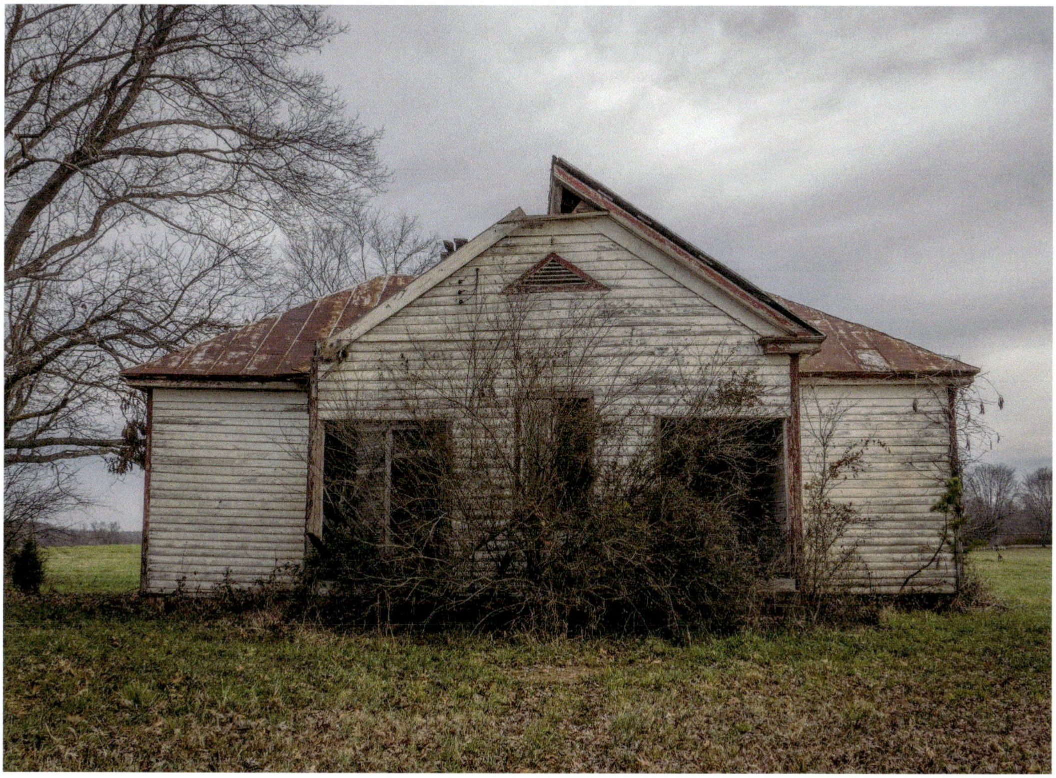

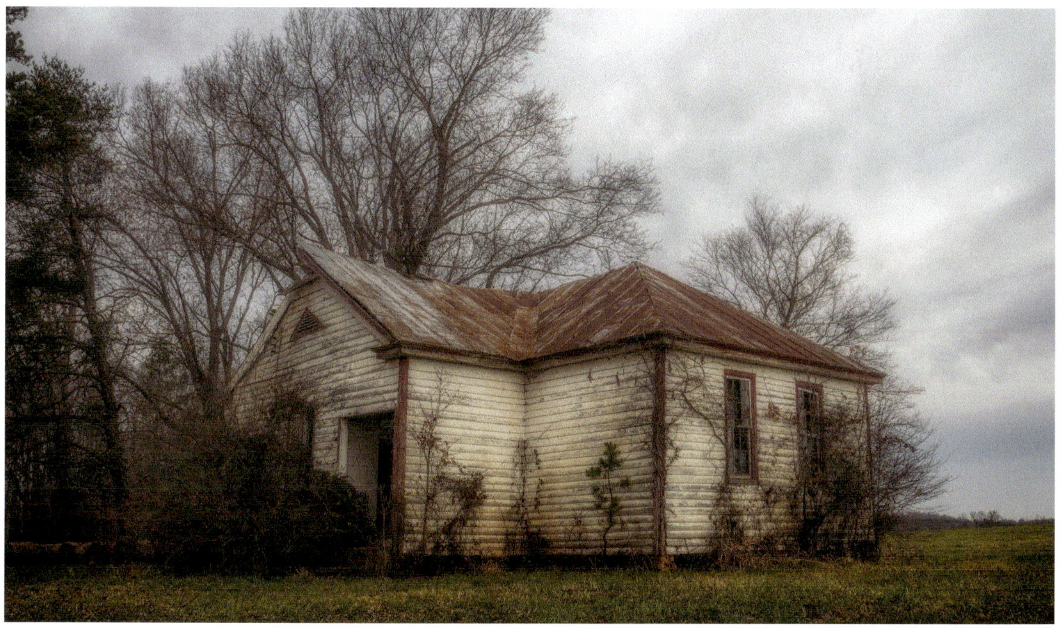

Photo 29: SECLUDED RUSTICATION: The front façade of an old building that I feel looks like it could be an old school. But, as we saw in Photo 24, I could be mistaken in my assumption. If you look closely, you can barely see the old sidewalk leading up to the front of the building.

Photo 30: THE OLD COUNTRY SCHOOL: An angled shot of the same building shown in Photo 29.

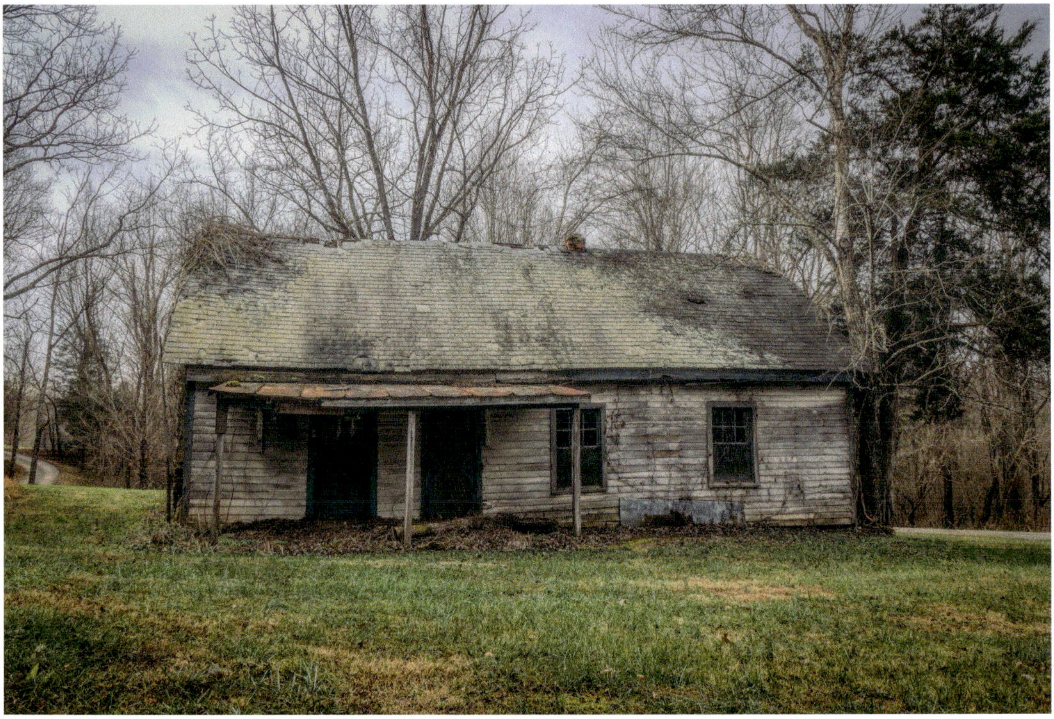

Photo 31: THE TAVERN HOUSE: The old building whose owner was gracious enough to allow me to photograph, whose grandparents once lived in it.

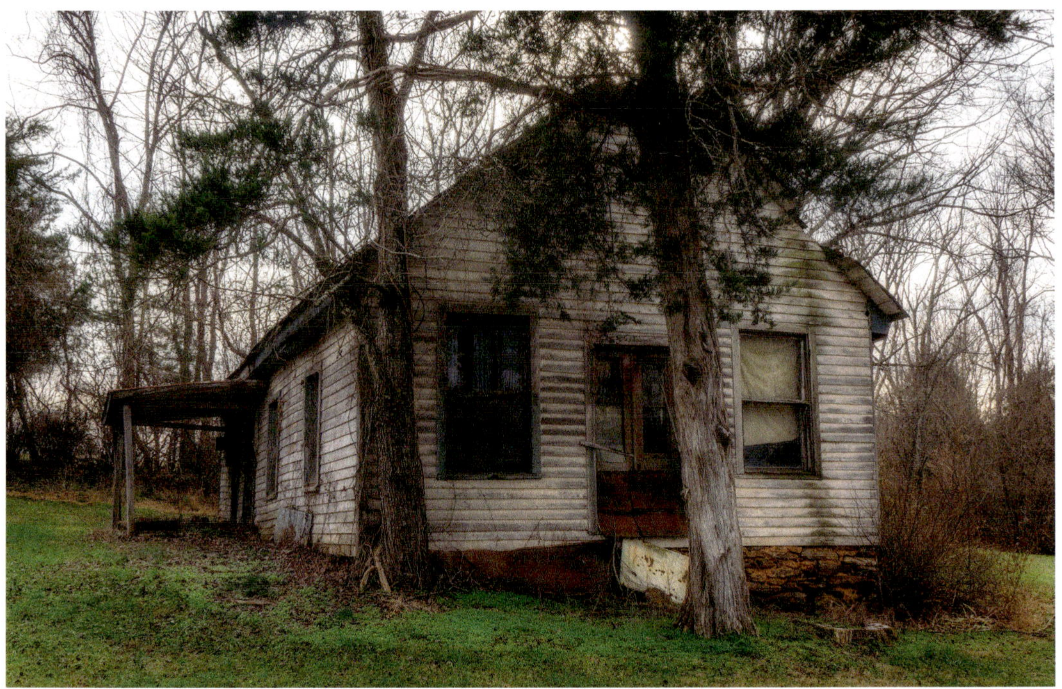

Photo 32: SIDE OF THE TAVERN HOUSE: As can be derived from my incredibly creative title, this is a photo of the side of the building shown in Photo 31.

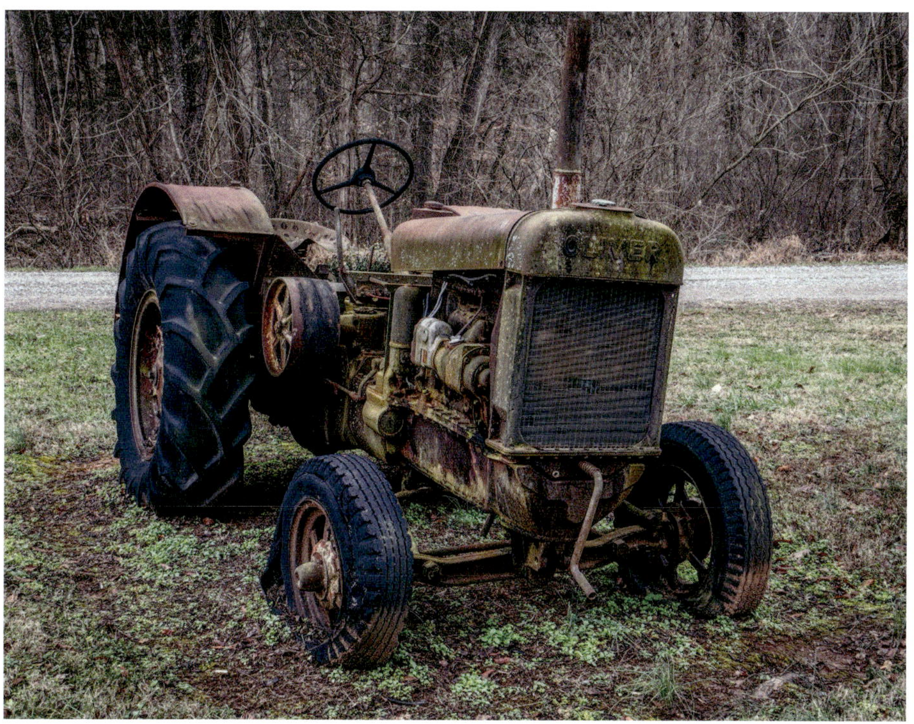

Photo 33: Tractor Supplies Needed: An old tractor that sits just behind the building in Photos 31 and 32.

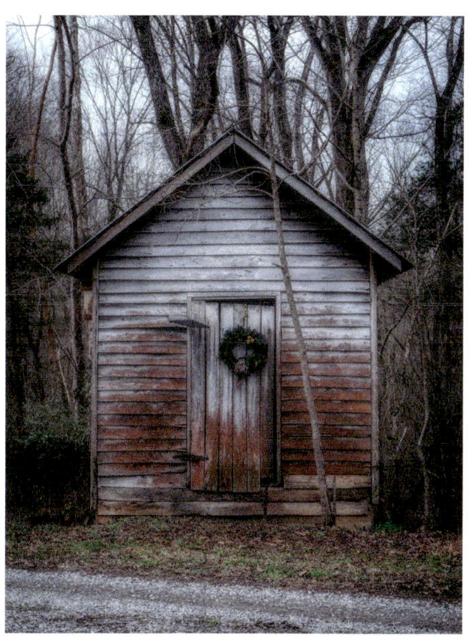

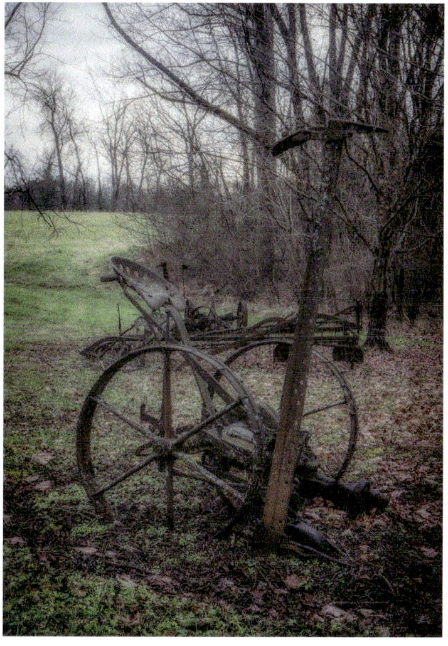

Above left: Photo 34: The Christmas Shack: I am not sure if that wreath is always there or if it was put up for Christmas (I took this photo a few weeks before Christmas), but I feel like it really makes the picture!

Above right: Photo 35: Remnant of Harvests of Old: Some old, rusting farm equipment sitting behind the building shown in Photos 31 and 32.

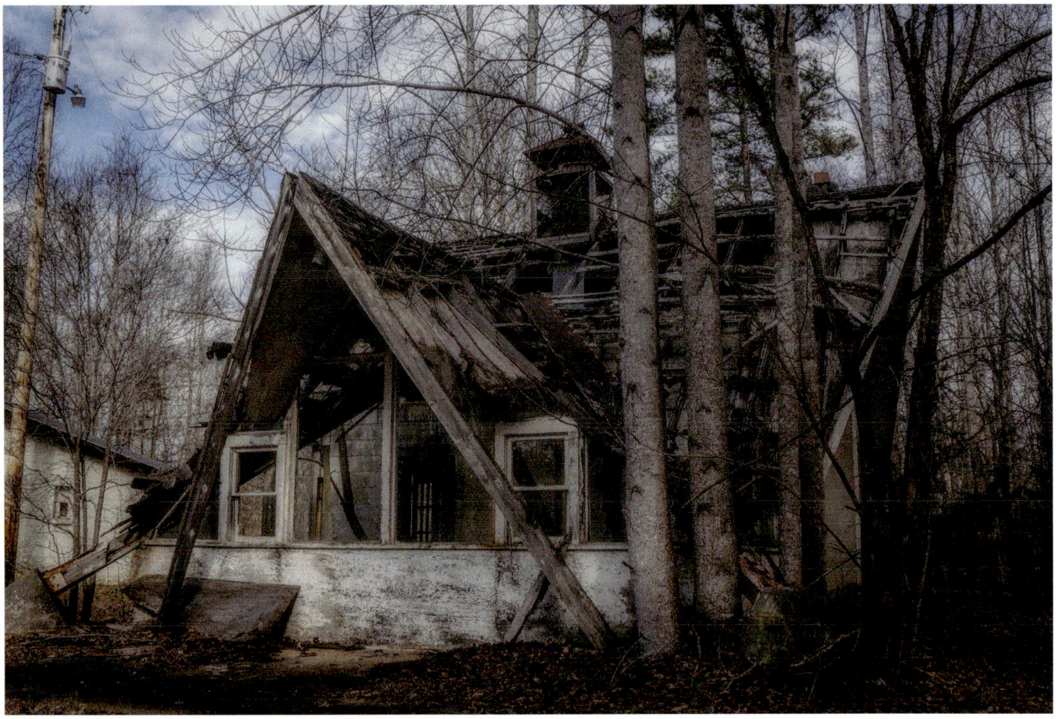

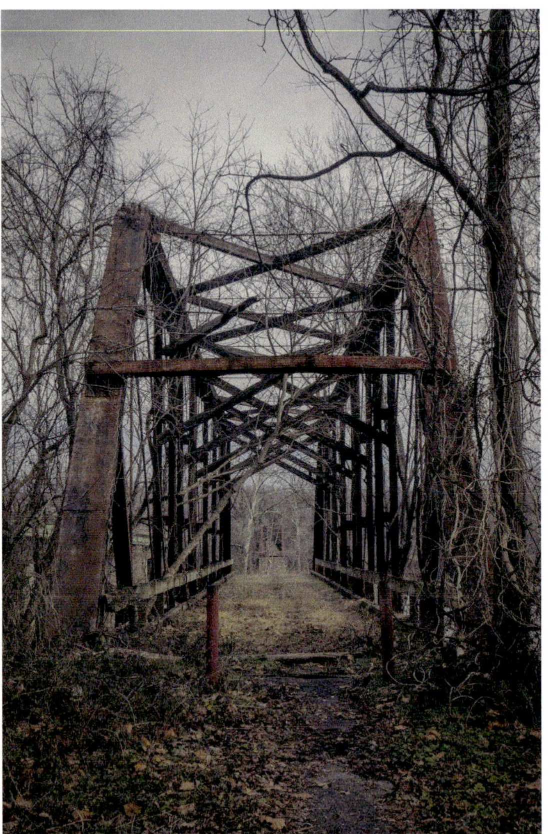

Above: Photo 36: ROUTE 250 TRADING POST: All that's left of what used to be, I'm sure, a popular stop along the well-traveled Route 250.

Left: Photo 37: BRIDGE TO NOWHERE: One of two sides of the former bridge that once spanned the James River at Cartersville. If you look closely, you can see part of the modern-day bridge peeking through the trees on the left side of the photo as well as the northern part of the old bridge near the center of the photo.

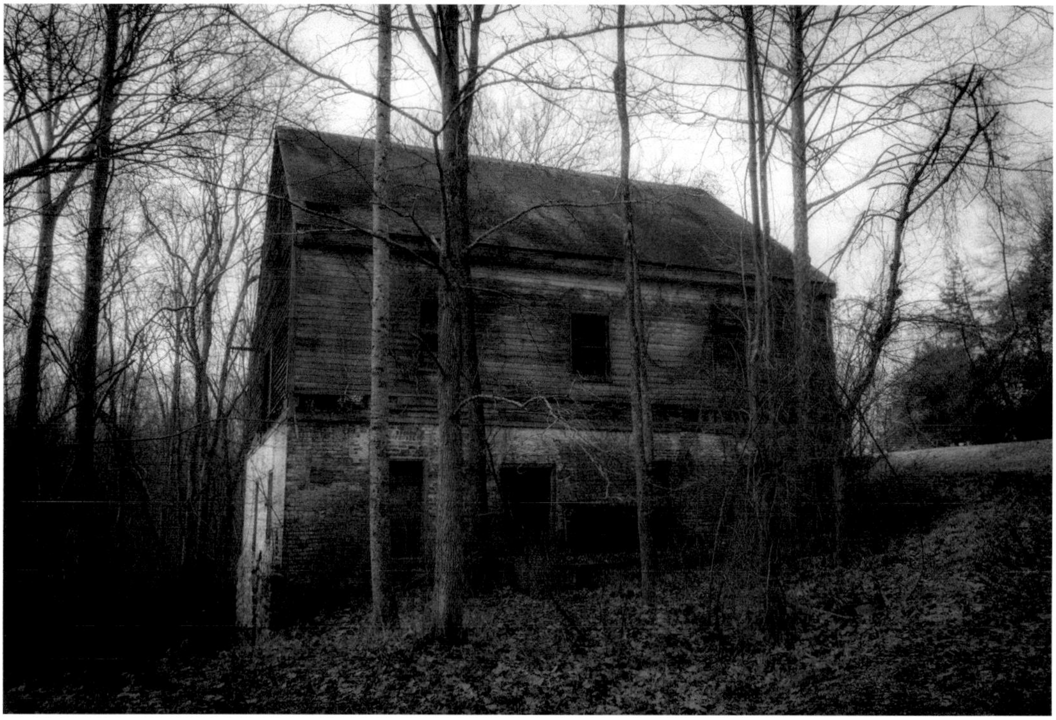

Photo 38: THE OLD MILL AT TRICE'S LAKE: One side of the old Flannagan's Mill.

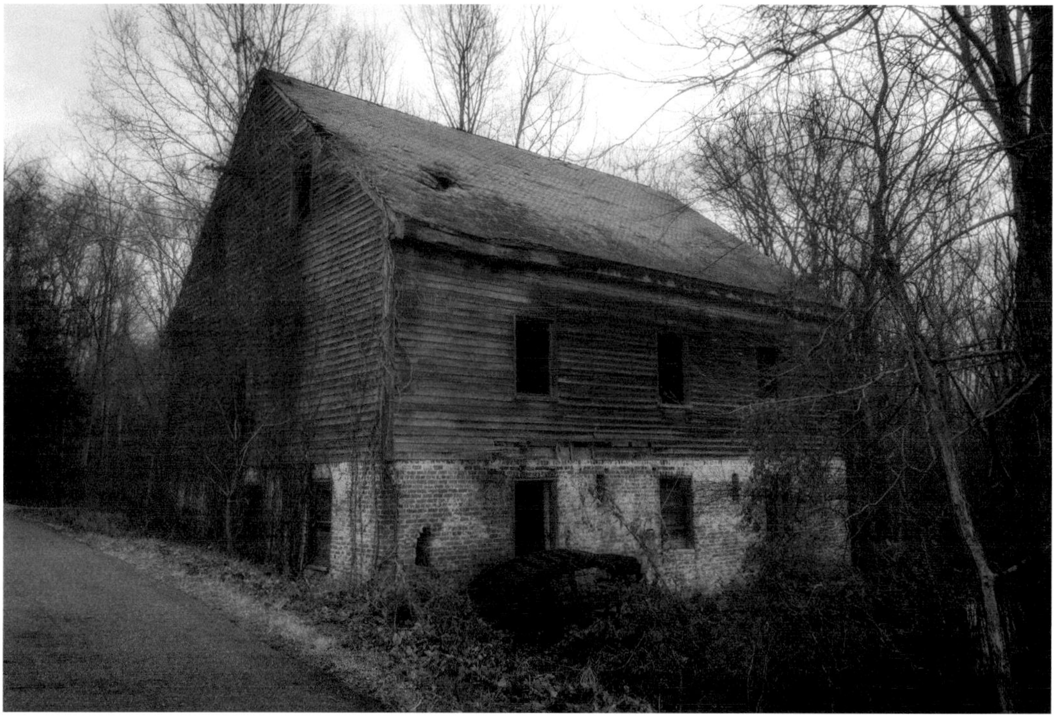

Photo 39: TRICE'S LAKE MILL: The other side of the mill shown in Photo 38. On this side you can still see the old water wheel.

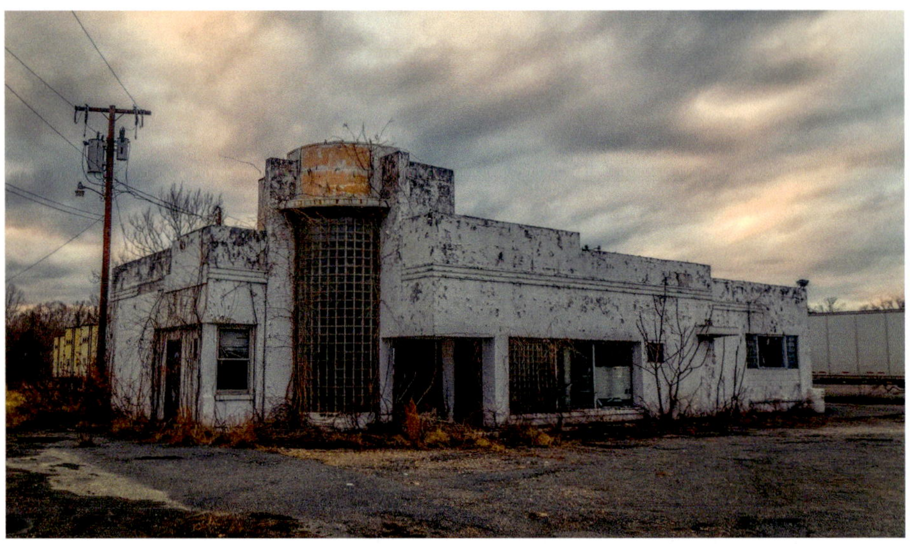

Photo 40: No Business as Usual: The remnants of an old truck stop that later became the office of a trucking company.

A few days later, I took my two oldest kids with me to the home of one of my sisters. While there, she and her two children led us back into the woods behind their house about half a mile to the spot where an old Dodge car had once been abandoned. I whipped out my camera and got a photo (Photo 41). Then they led us about another quarter of a mile to a little old house that had not been lived in for years (Photo 42).

A month later, I convinced my family to go on another long drive with me out to the town of Moneta. I desperately wanted to photograph the two buildings in Photos 43 and 44. If you are a fan of movies from the '90s, then these buildings may look a little familiar to you. Both of these buildings were used in the movie *What About Bob?* (1991). The building in Photo 43 was portrayed as the general store and the other was portrayed as the bus depot. At one time these buildings were located on the main road that passed through Moneta. However, in the year 2000, a bypass was completed that would take travelers around the town instead of through it. To make matters worse, what had been the main road through town was permanently closed at the railroad tracks creating dead ends at the tracks on both halves of the now divided road.

Photos 45–52 were also taken that day in and around the little town of Moneta.

I saw the two houses in Photos 53 and 54 one day after work as I was driving to my daughter's softball game. They were sitting right next to each other. I found a safe spot to park and made sure no cars were coming before I stood in the road to photograph them.

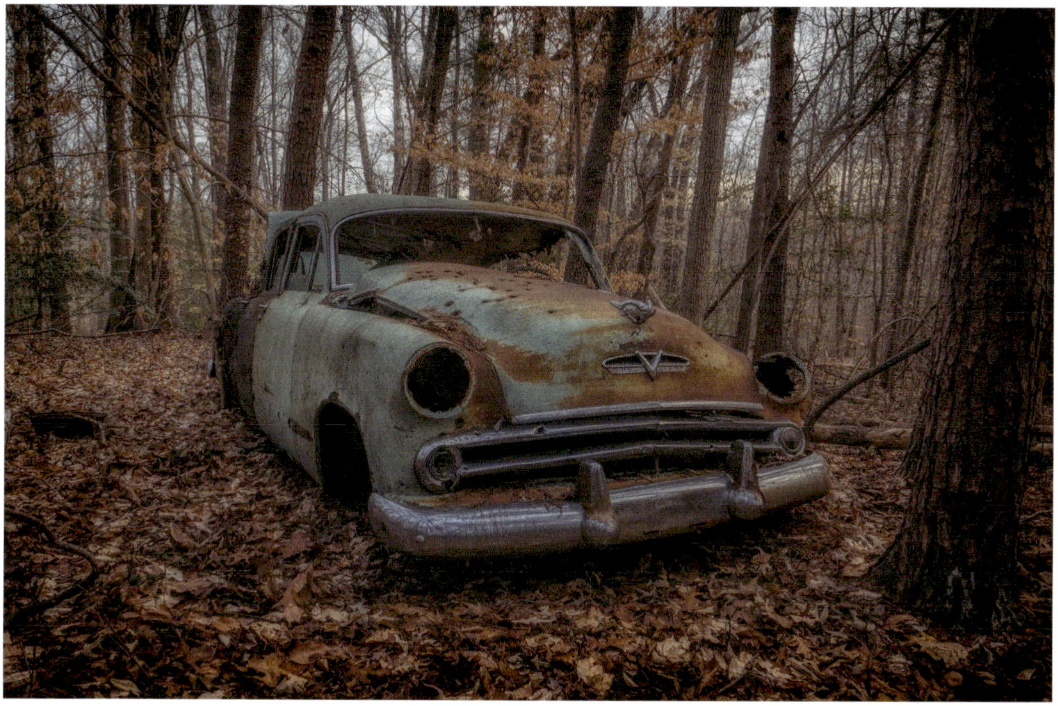

Photo 41: HIDDEN AND WASTING AWAY: The old car back in the woods behind my sister's house out in the country. Another case that makes me wonder just how long ago this car was last driven and parked in this location.

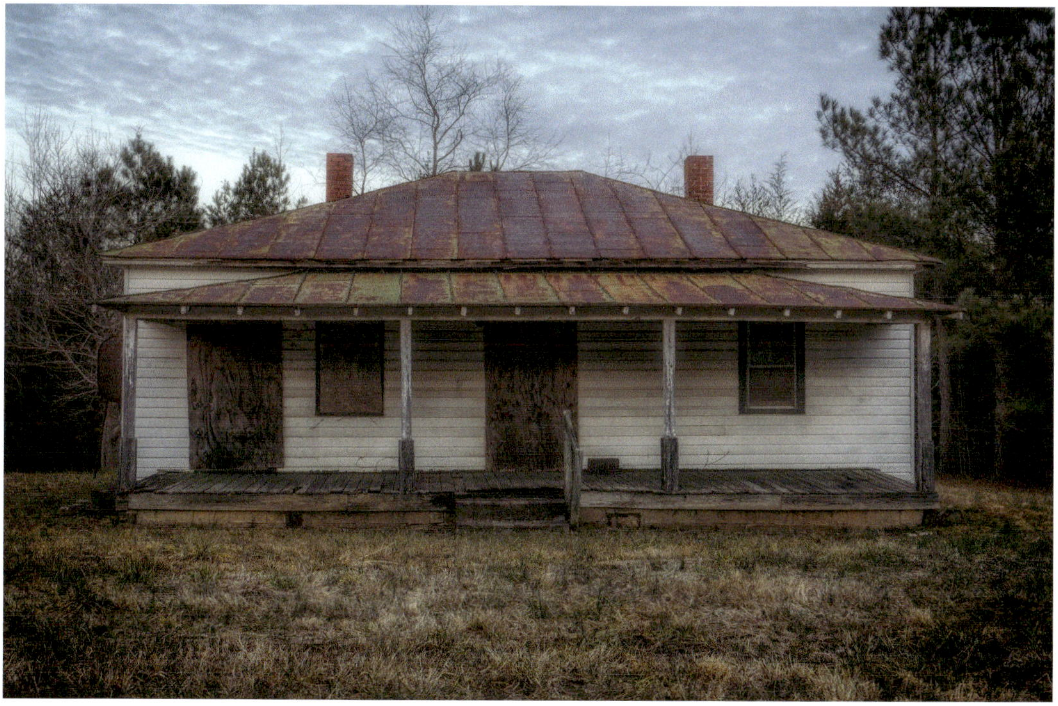

Photo 42: CABIN IN THE CLEARING: According to my sister and her children, this house had a much more rustic look to it before someone boarded up the doors and windows.

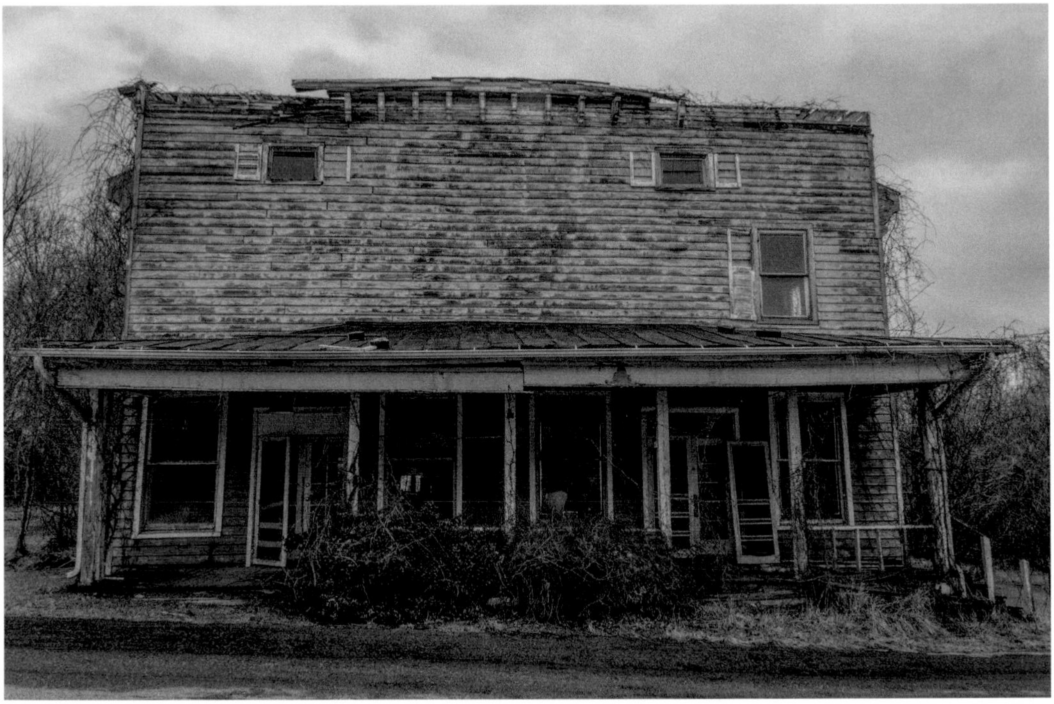

Photo 43: WHAT ABOUT WINNIPESAUKEE GENERAL STORE?: One of the two buildings in Moneta that was featured in the movie *What About Bob?*

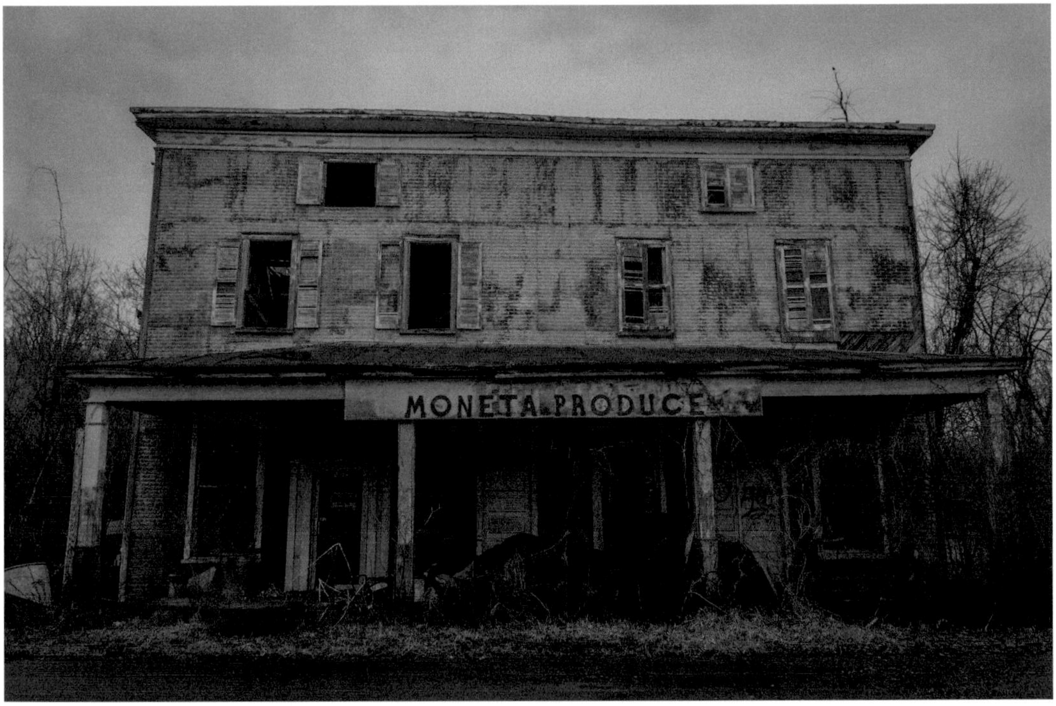

Photo 44: MONETA PRODUCE: Sitting next to the building in Photo 43, this building was portrayed as the bus depot in the movie *What About Bob?*

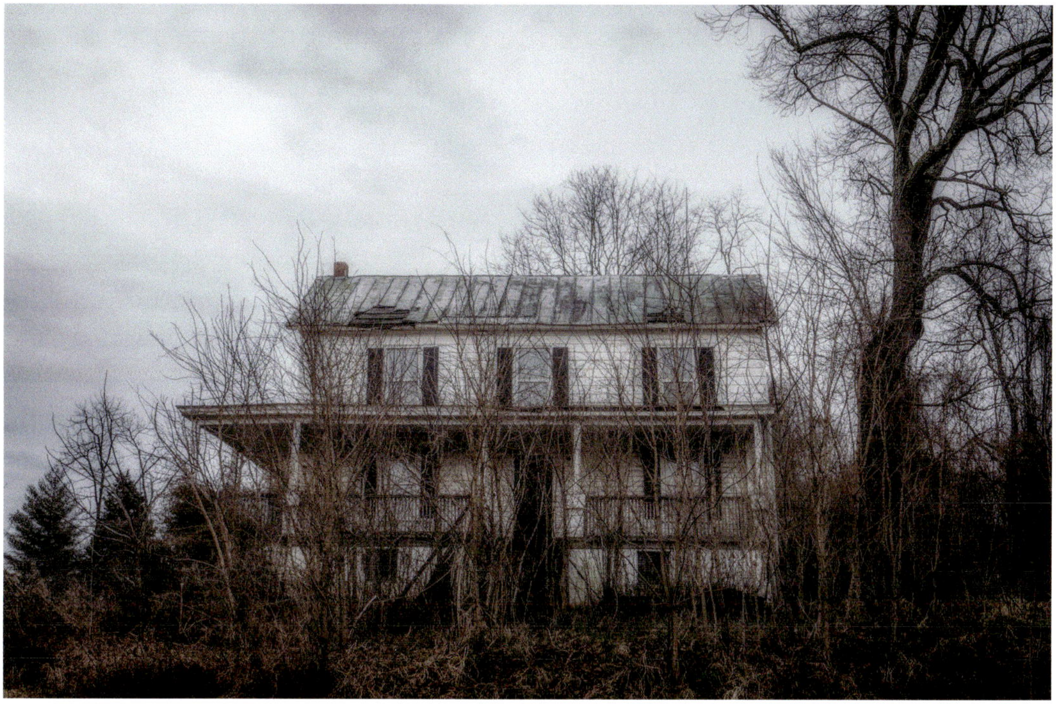

Photo 45: THE HOUSE ON THE HILL: An abandoned home in the town of Moneta. This home has been demolished since this photo was taken.

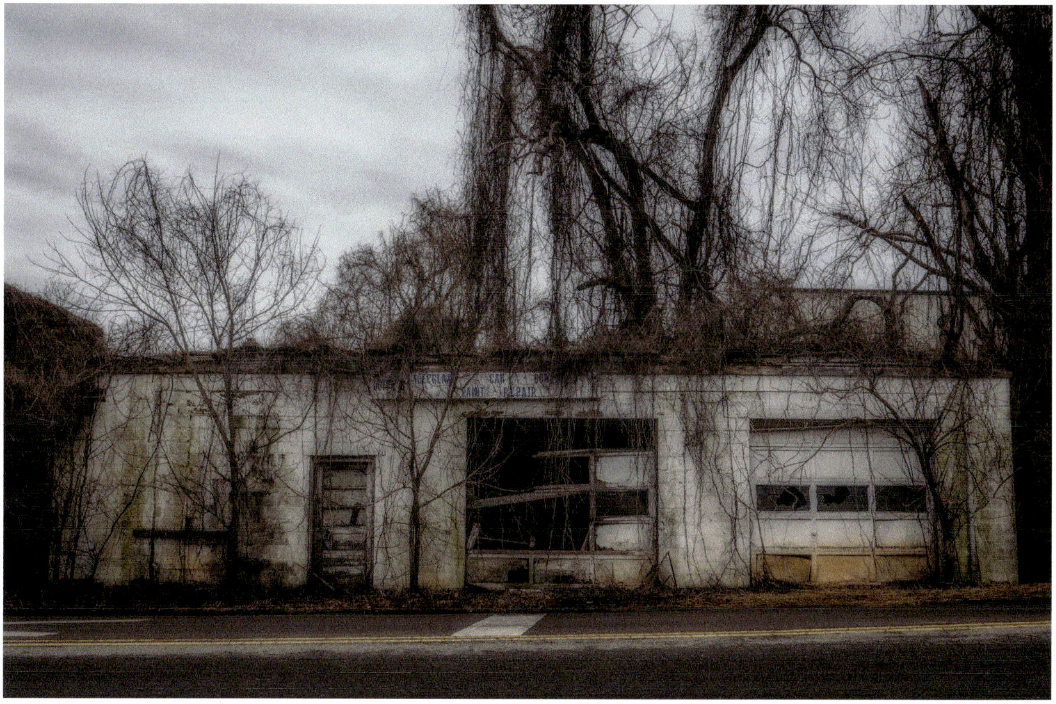

Photo 46: OUT OF SERVICE STATION: An old, abandoned garage also in the town of Moneta.

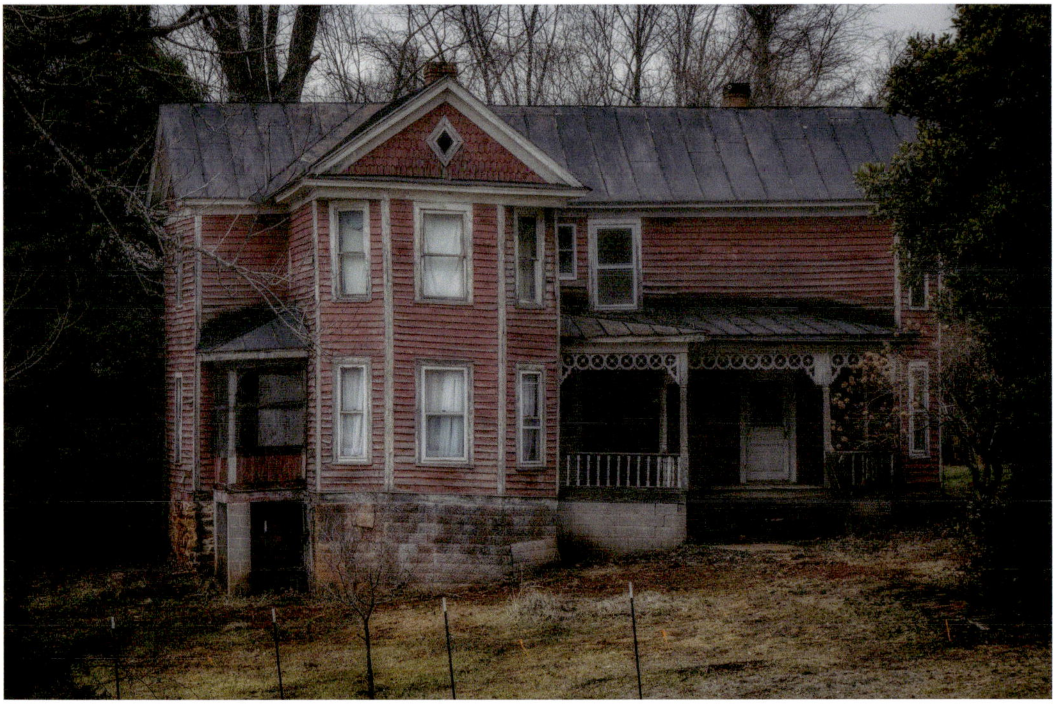

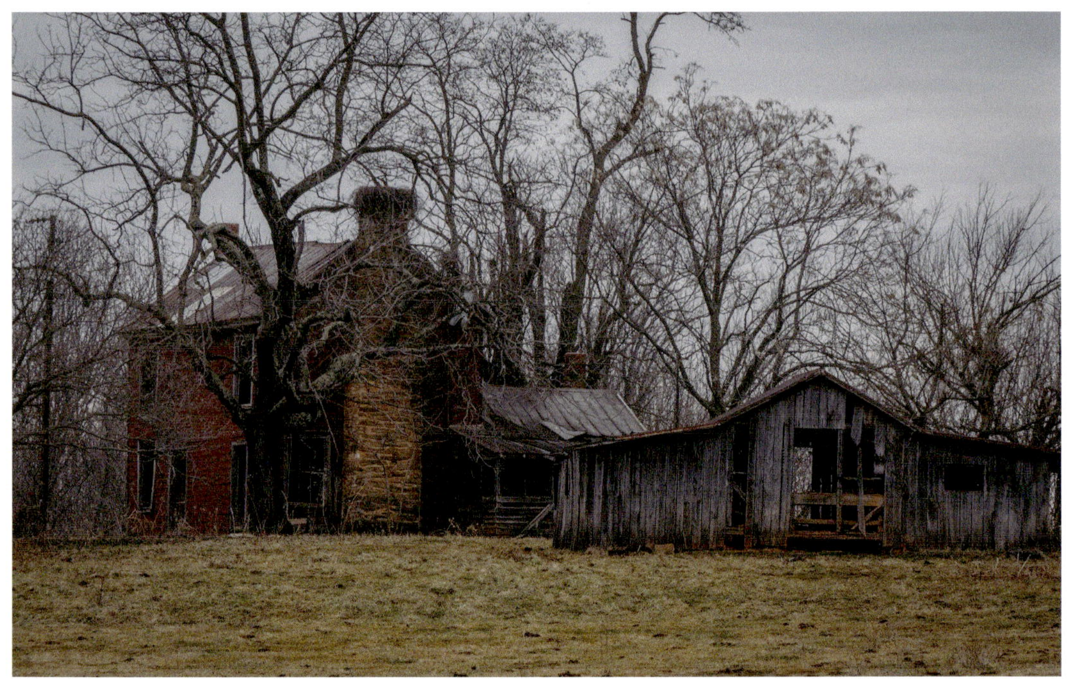

Photo 47: THE FORGOTTEN FARMHOUSE: An old home not far from the town of Moneta. This home has since been demolished.

Photo 48: DISTANT MEMORIES: I gave this photo that name because I took this shot from down the road a "distance" using my telephoto lens. This old farmhouse, however, is still standing, but just barely.

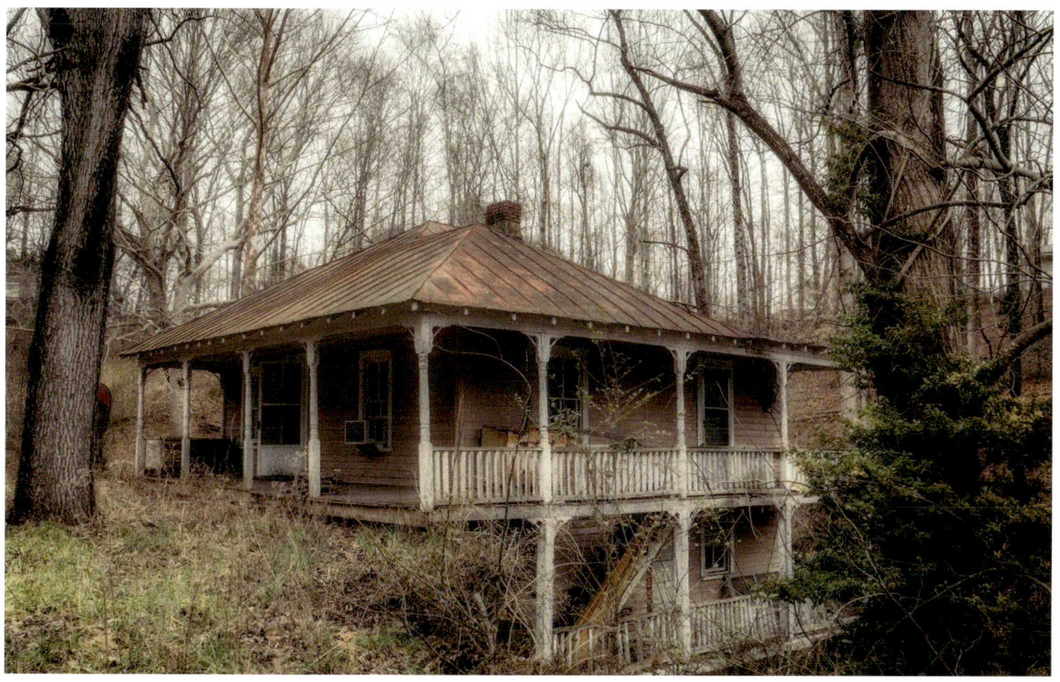

Photo 49: Layered House: I first discovered this home back in 2012 and photographed it (it was even abandoned back then), but once I got the photo up on my computer, I discovered it was out of focus. I am glad that I was able to photograph it again nearly a decade later.

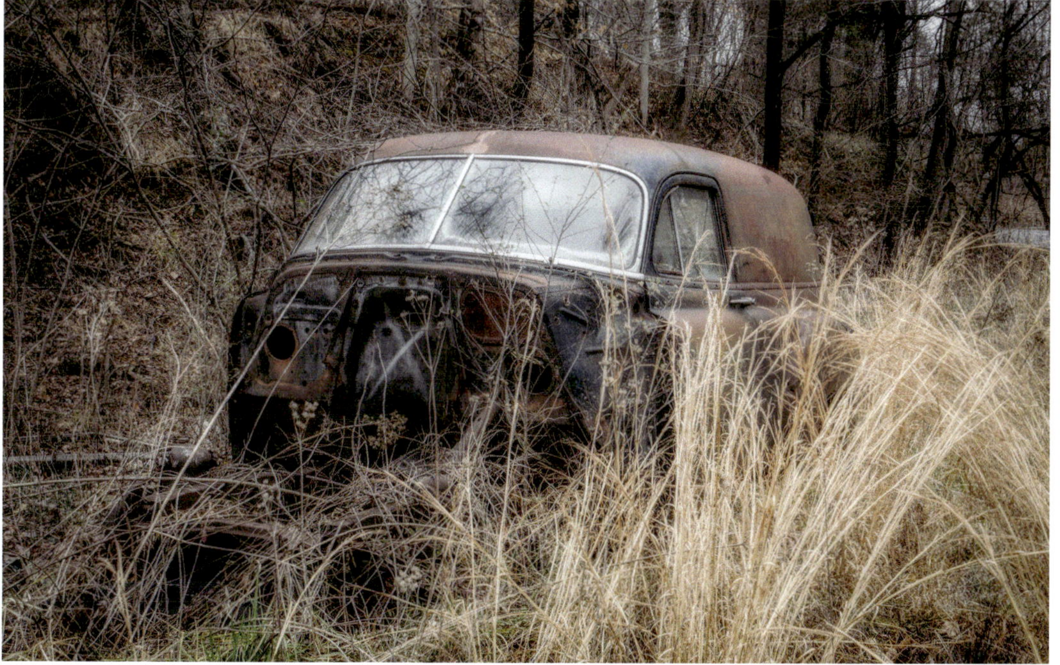

Photo 50: Waiting in the Weeds: This vehicle and the one in Photo 51 are sitting in a small clearing across the road from the house in Photo 49. They were also both there back in 2012, but my photos of them from back then were also out of focus. I made sure to use a tripod this time!

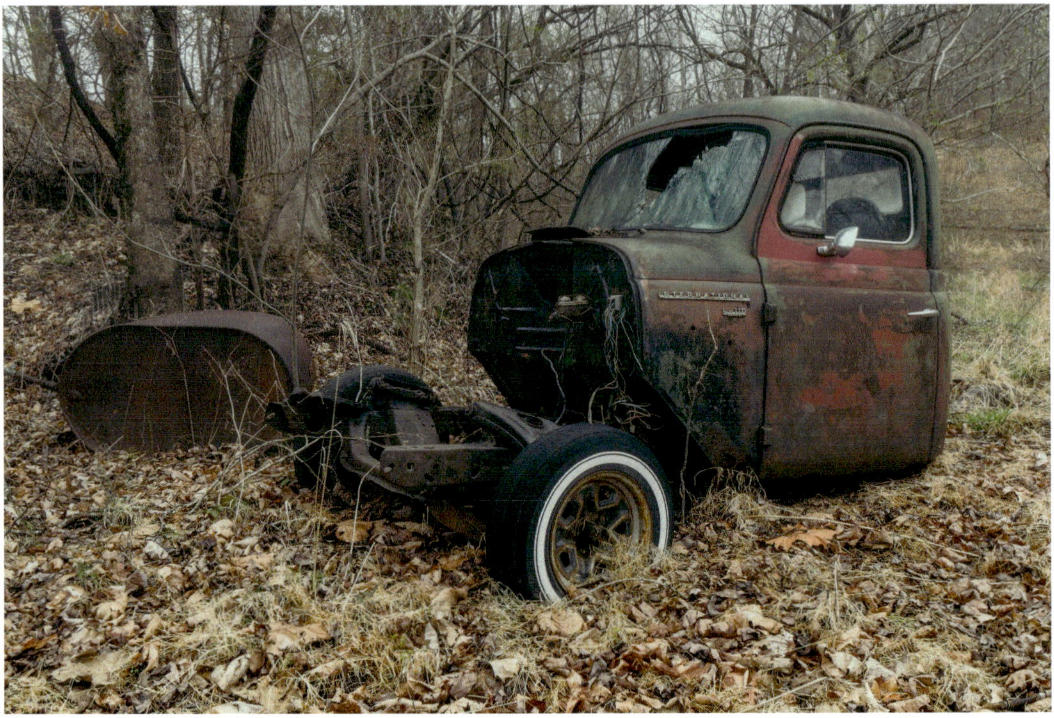

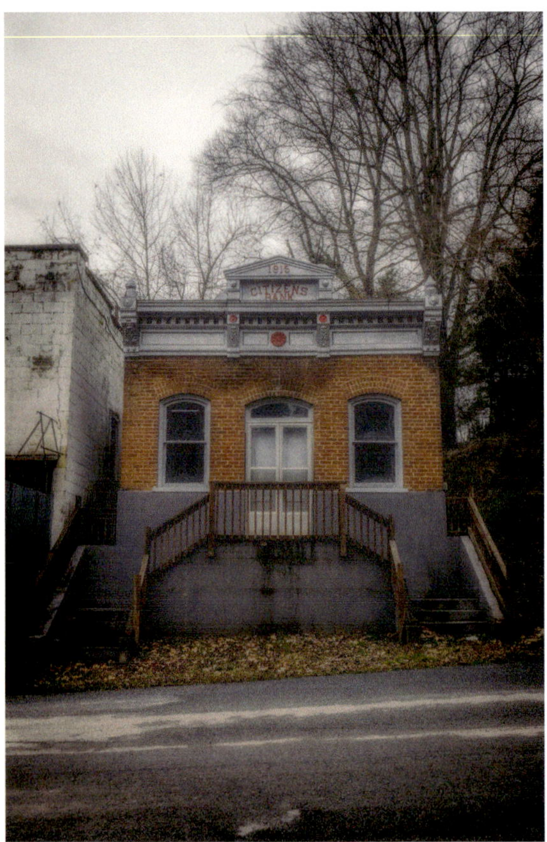

Above: Photo 51: INTERNATIONAL DISASTER: The other vehicle that sits across from the home in Photo 49.

Left: Photo 52: CITIZENS BANK 1915: Opened in 1915 in the small town of Huddleston, this bank was an unfortunate victim of the Great Depression. Since then, it has been home to various shops and businesses. It was in the process of being renovated at one time, but by the looks of it on Google Street View, I do not know if that is still the case.

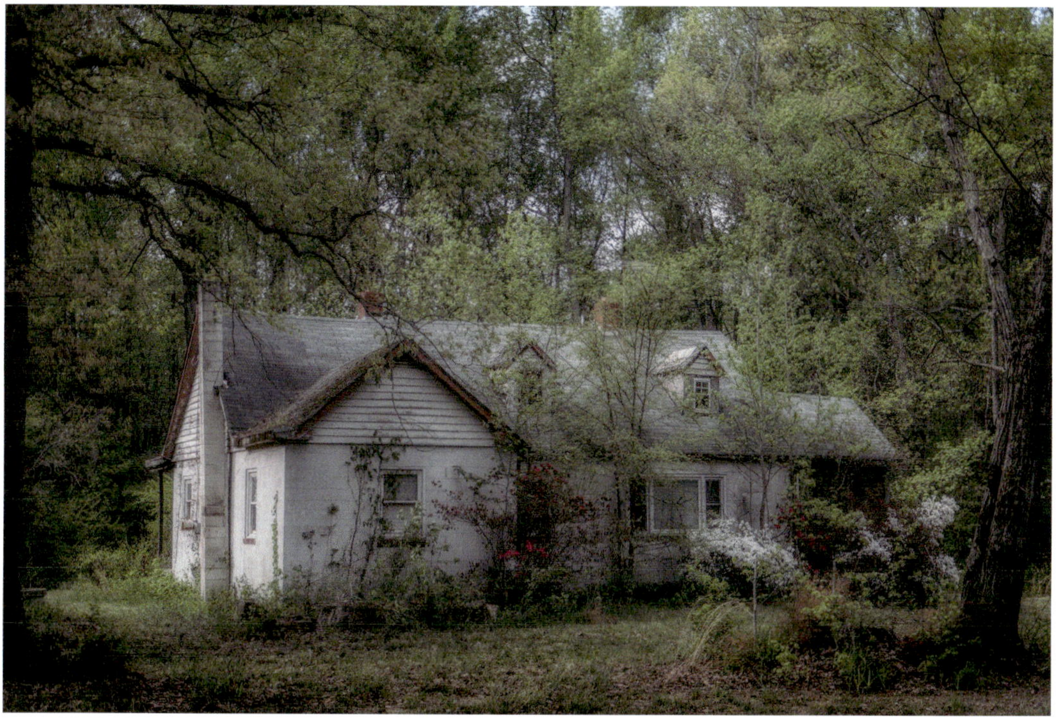

Photo 53: COTTAGE IN THE WOODS: A quaint little home that I passed on the way to one of my daughter's softball games after work one day.

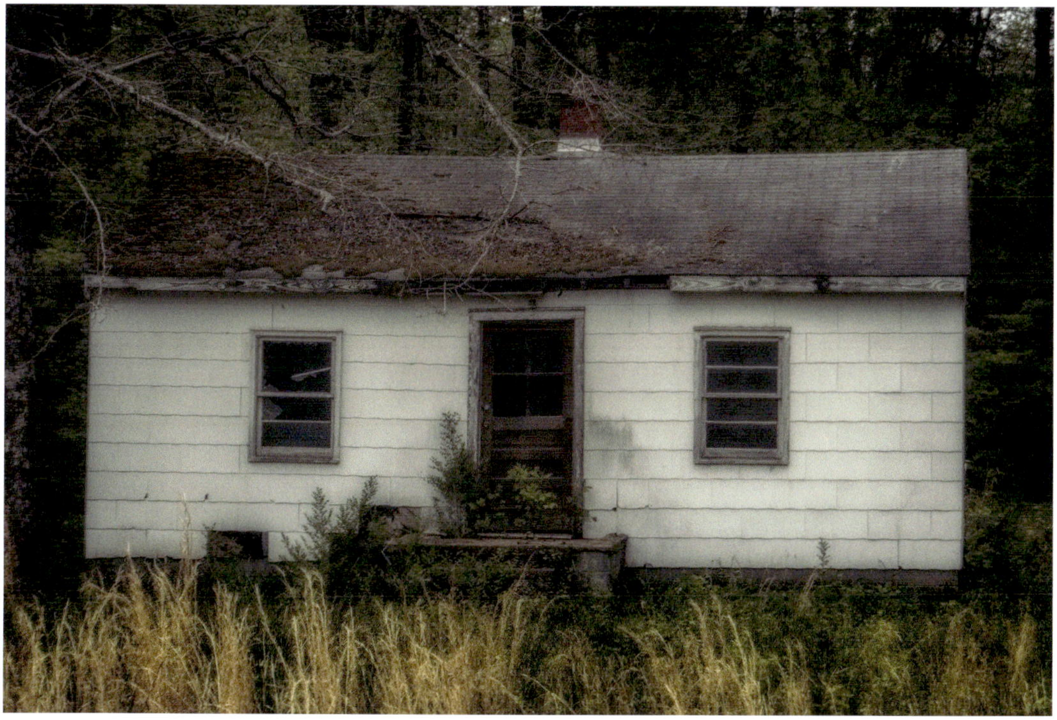

Photo 54: THE DISREMEMBERED CABIN: This small little home sits next to the one in Photo 53.

I got so wrapped up with beginning this story in early 2020 that I forgot about some photos that I had taken at the end of 2019. I had already turned in all of the materials for *Forgotten Virginia* earlier that year, so these shots did not make it into that book. My wife and I took a weekend trip to the Outer Banks of North Carolina for our wedding anniversary. We drove down Route 460 on the way back—it was a nice overcast day—and since I knew that we would be passing by some houses and buildings that I wanted to capture on camera, my wife was gracious enough to allow me to do so. I only knew about the house in Photo 55 because I had taken a wrong turn once down the street on which it sits. Photos 56–60 were also taken that afternoon as we continued on Route 460.

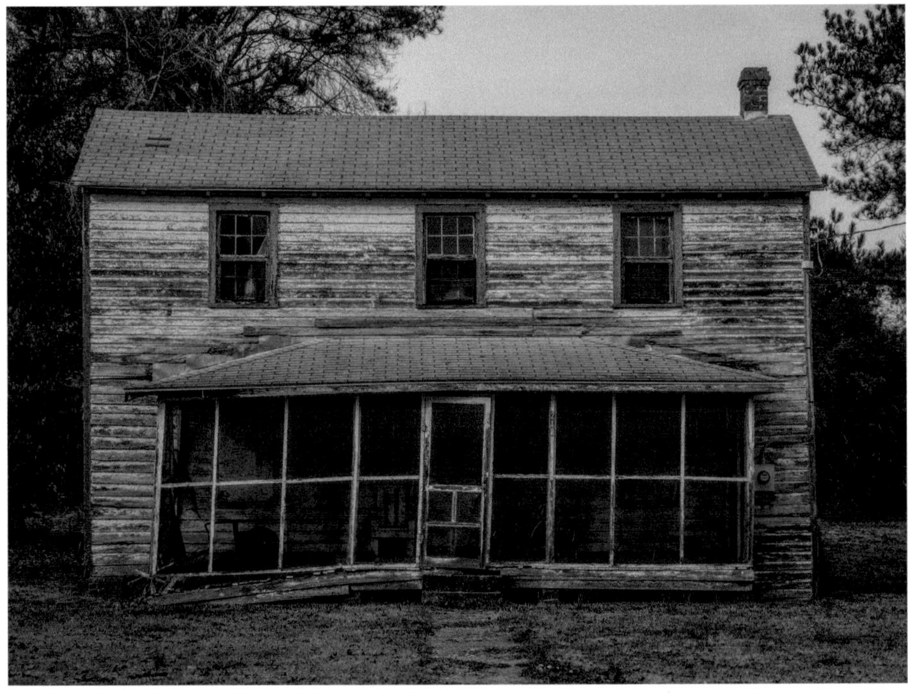

Photo 55: THE HOUSE DOWN THE BLOCK: The home that I only discovered because I took a wrong turn once down the road on which it sits.

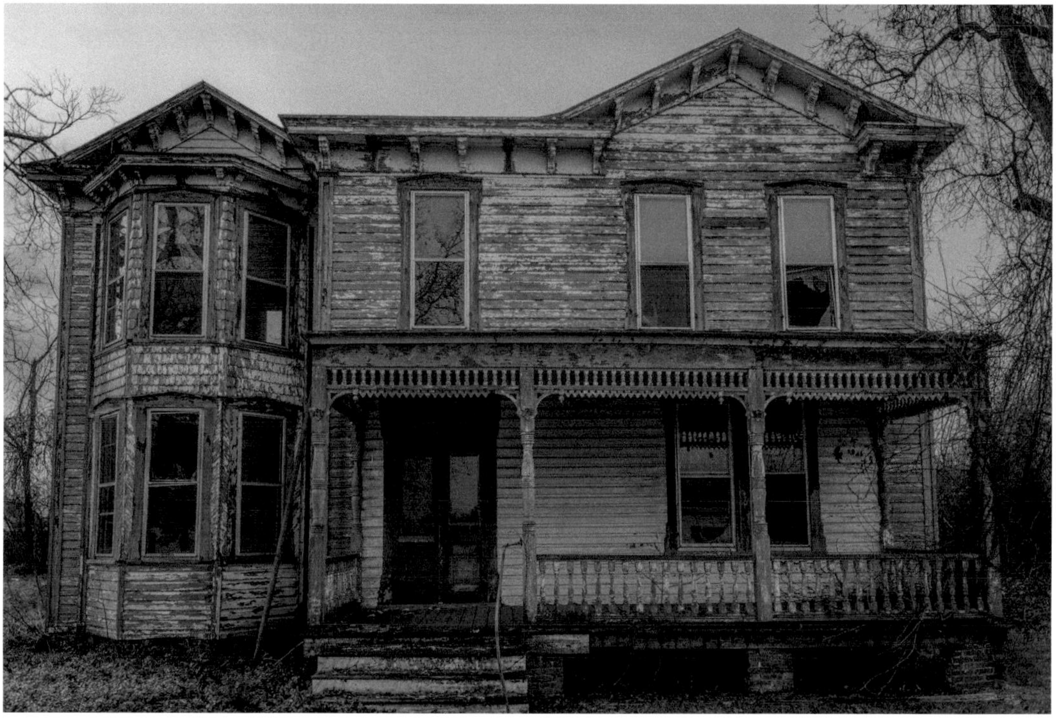

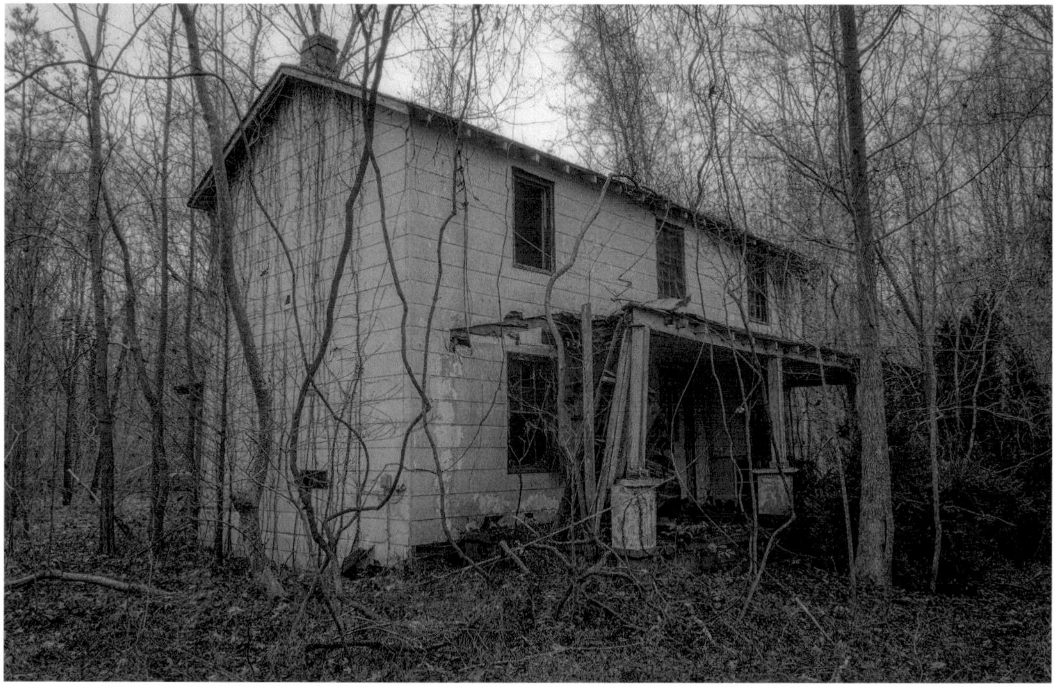

Photo 56: Reminiscence of Grandeur: This old home now has a fresh look on life as it has been renovated since taking this photo.

Photo 57: Old Yella: This home sits right next to Route 460 but can only be seen once the leaves have fallen from the trees.

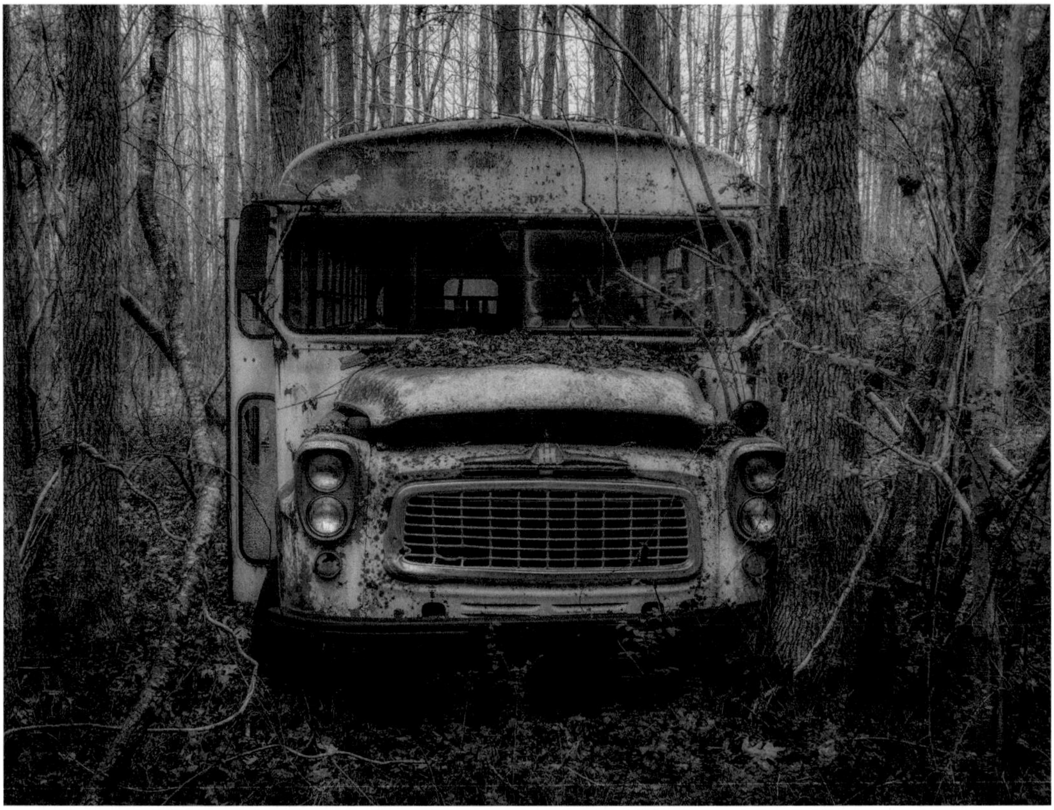

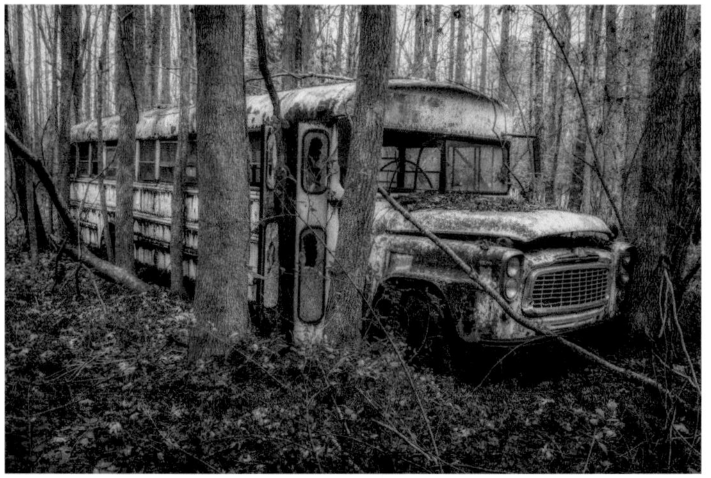

Photo 58: ᴇɴᴅ ᴏꜰ ᴛʜᴇ Lɪɴᴇ: Sitting a little way to the side of the home in Photo 57, this old bus seems to have been parked in its location years ago before the woods in which it now resides even existed because you can see how the trees have literally grown around it.

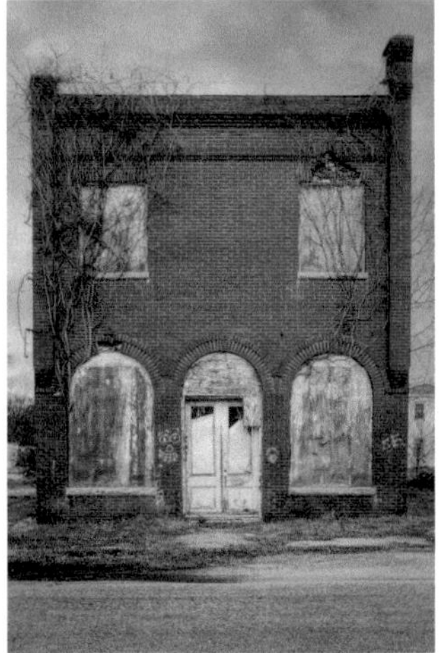

Above left: Photo 59: Pᴇʀᴍᴀɴᴇɴᴛ Bᴜs Sᴛᴏᴘ: A side view of the bus in Photo 58. The trees almost look like natural prison bars keeping the bus trapped in the spot where someone, years ago, parked it and never drove it again.

Above right: Photo 60: Eᴍᴘᴛʏ ᴀɴᴅ Fᴏʀʟᴏʀɴ: An old building sits unused and abandoned in the small town of Disputanta.

The unfinished house in Photos 61–63 is an interesting one. It is so well hidden in the trees that I literally had passed by this house twice daily for more than fifteen years and never knew it was there. Its story is intriguing, but also sad. Back in the 1940s, a gentleman began building what was to be his and his wife's dream house where they would live when he retired. I have not found any actual documentation on the following, but I have seen where others have said that before he finished the house his wife passed away. He then decided that he would complete the home for himself and for his mother to live in together. Yet, once again, before he could complete the house his mother also passed away. It was at that point that he stopped working on it and abandoned the house. Whether that was the actual cause for the house being left unfinished I cannot say, but the house was sold in the early 1960s and has sat incomplete ever since.

The two barns in Photos 64 and 65 lie on land that I presume was once a working farm. There was a farmhouse nearby, but I was not able to see much of it at all, let alone approach it. It was completely surrounded by what seemed to be a rogue patch of bamboo. There was no other bamboo in the area, just around the house, almost as if it had been planted that way on purpose. It was so thick that I could not even begin to work my way through it. So, I took some photos of the two barns and went on my way. I have recently seen where the local jurisdiction has given approval for a shopping center to be built on that land.

After the Civil War, the Jackson Ward neighborhood in downtown Richmond became a thriving African American community. However, in the 1950s, Interstate 95 was built through the center of the neighborhood, splitting it into two halves. One half continued to thrive, while the other did not do so well. On the day I took Photo 66, this home sat alone on the portion of the block on which it is located. No doubt, many other homes just like it lined that street at one time. I learned that a few months after I took this photo a fire destroyed much of this home including the roof and most of the walls. Now, Google Street View shows the front facade and remaining external side wall being held up by various supporting boards and the home surrounded by a small chain link fence.

Photos 67 and 68 were a lunch-hour outing. I already had the church marked on Google Maps, so I drove over to it and got this shot. It was a cloudy and misty day which added to the character of the photo. I then decided to drive up the same road to see what I could find. I happened upon the old home in Photo 68. I stopped my car right there in the road, rolled down my window, and took the shot. I did not notice the buzzards on the chimney, however, until I was editing the photo in post-processing.

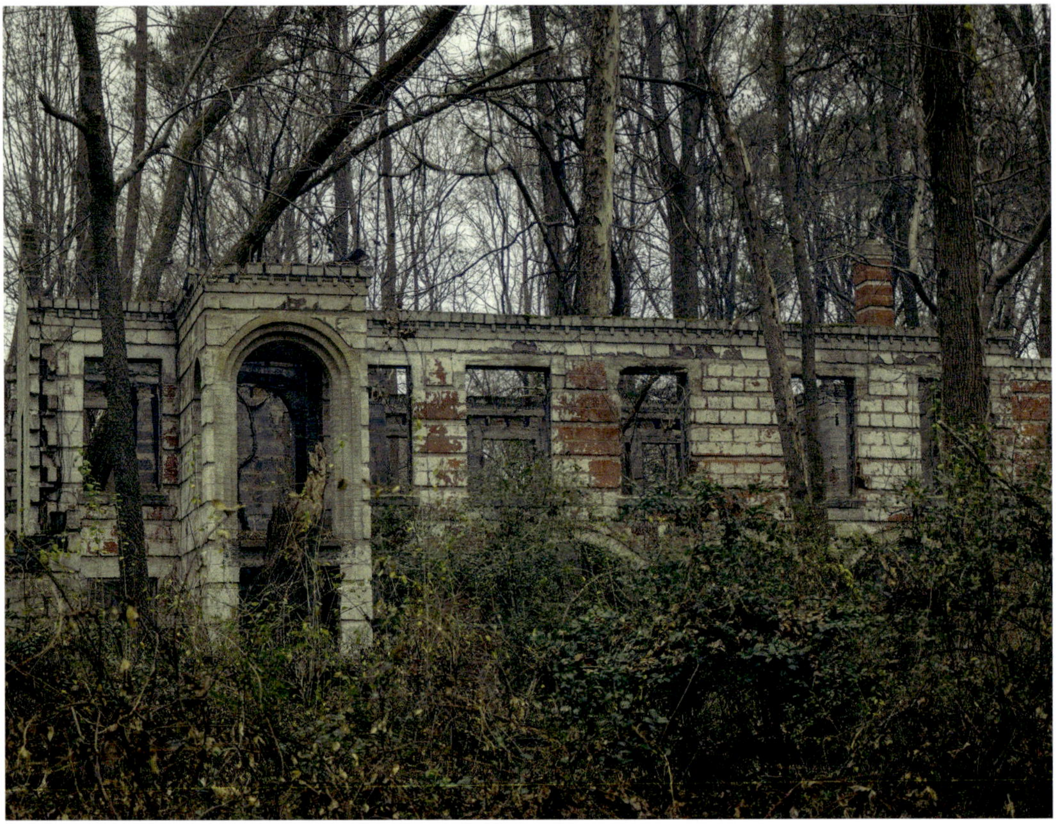

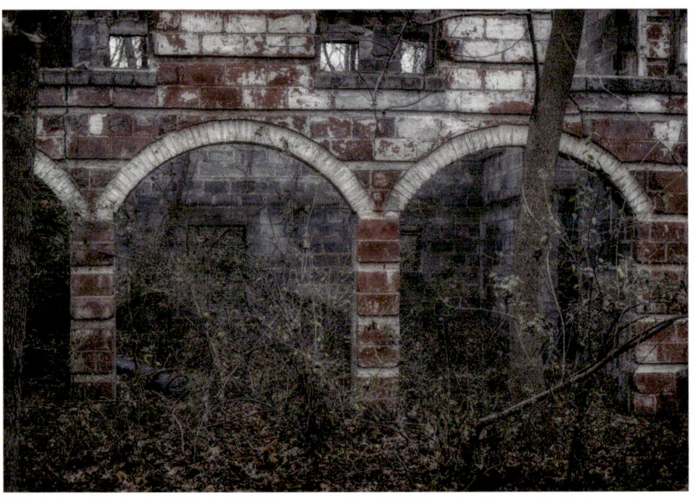

Photo 61: Unfinished and Forsaken: The unfinished home, hidden among the trees, that was begun sometime in the 1940s but never completed.

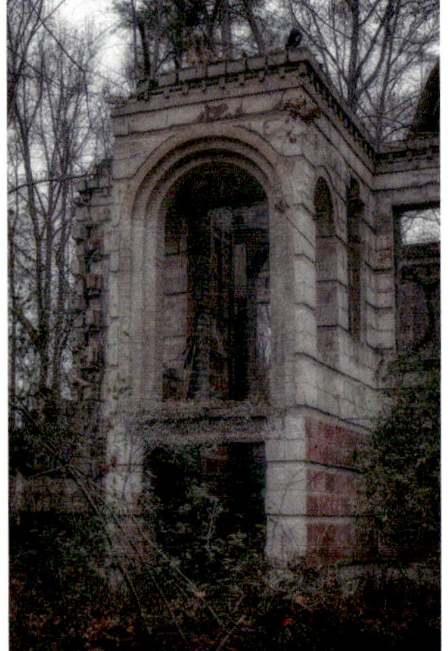

Above left: Photo 62: Castle Arches: A portion of the home in Photo 61. The arches, which were going to be entrances to a garage, make it seem almost castle-like.

Above right: Photo 63: The Castle Entrance: A close-up shot of what was meant to be the grand front entrance to the home in Photo 61.

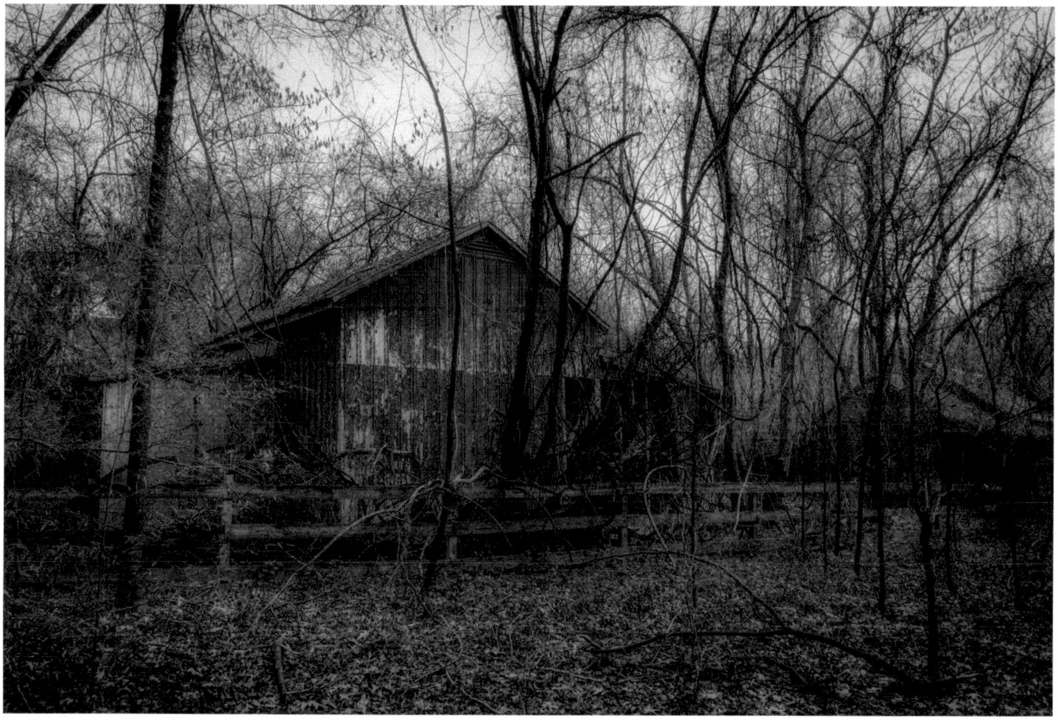

Photo 64: Barns in the Woods: Two barns on what was once a farm that I came across one day. The nearby farmhouse was completely inaccessible due to being surrounded by extremely dense bamboo.

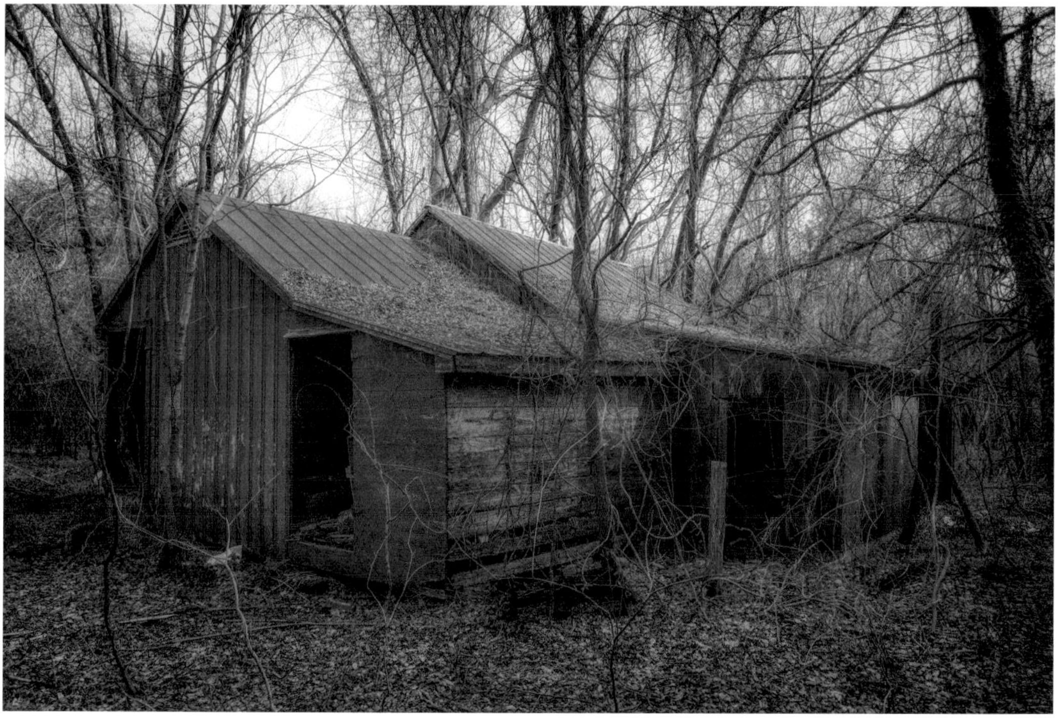

Photo 65: Secluded and Forgotten: The second of the two old barns from Photo 64.

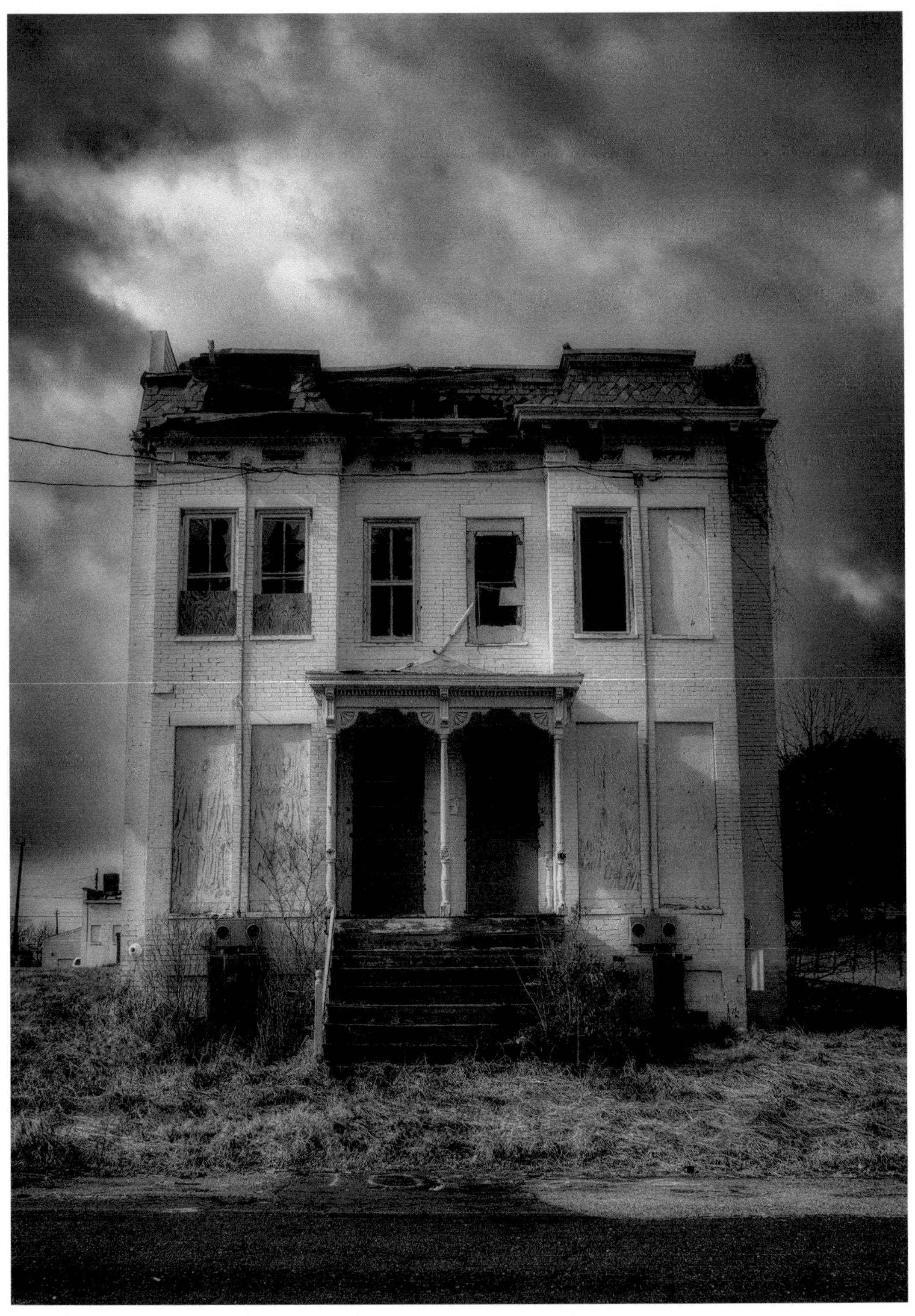

Photo 66: THE ROW HOUSE: A lonely secluded, and now mostly gone, home on the northern side of Richmond's Jackson Ward.

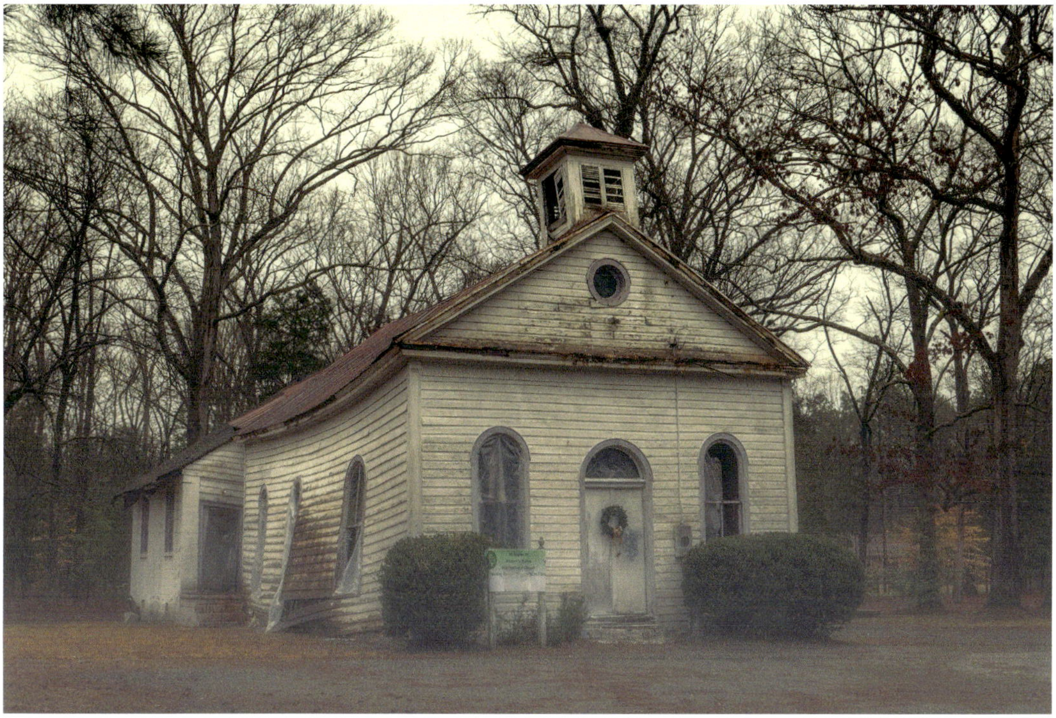

Photo 67: END OF SERMON: An old country church that has long since had its pews filled with parishioners.

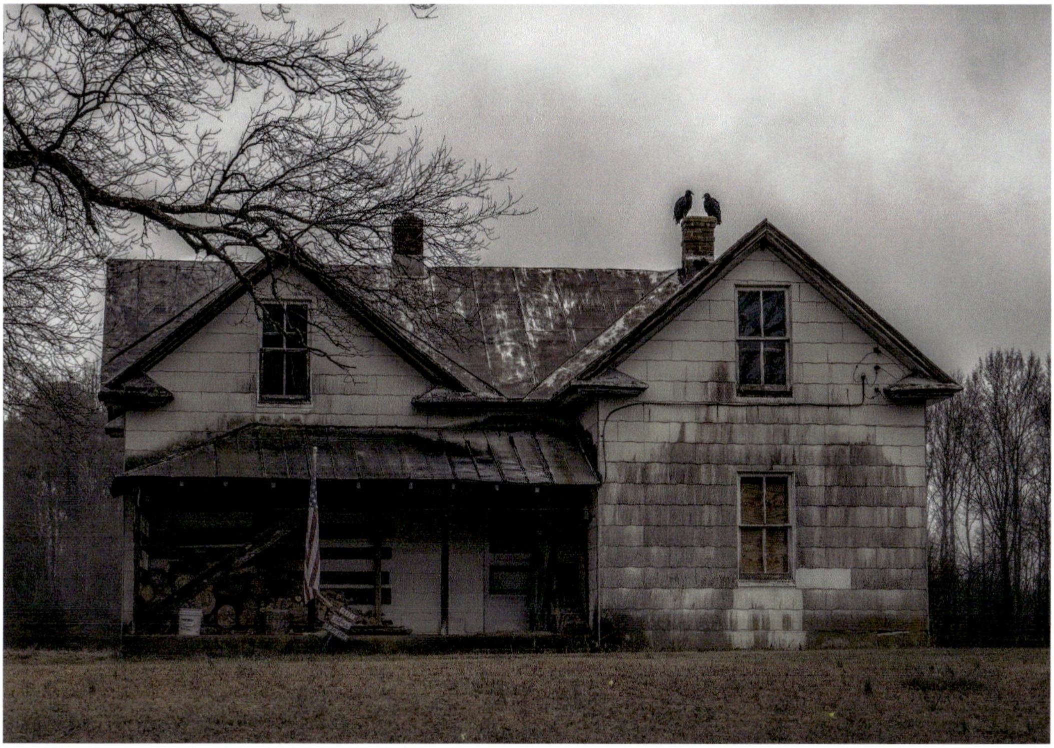

Photo 68: RUSTIC DEGRADATION: An old home not far from the church in Photo 67.

In March 2022, my family and I took a drive out to Luray Caverns. I already had the house in Photo 69 marked, and since it was along the way, we stopped so I could take a photo. But what I did not know at the time was that the houses in Photos 70 and 71 were just down the road. Over the years, I have seen many other people share photos and stories about the house in Photo 70; in fact, it seems to be quite well known. The stories all speak of the significance of the laundry hanging on the porch. Apparently if there was laundry hanging on the line, it was a signal that they had moonshine available for purchase and the colors of the laundry corresponded to different flavors of moonshine. I do not know what flavor a multi-color patchwork quilt corresponded to, however! As interesting as that story is, I was much more intrigued by the old house that sits next door, which is the one in Photo 71. I have seen it called the rainbow roof house. I do not know any stories about it, but to me it is a textbook example of what one would picture in their mind when imagining an old, abandoned Appalachian Mountain home. I imagine many evenings were spent sitting on that old front porch.

Photo 72 is one that was taken for my first volume of *Forgotten Virginia*, but for some reason I never used it in the book. Others have identified this school as the old Buckhorn High/Elementary School just outside of the ghost town of Union Level, VA. It began as a high school and was later an elementary school. Apparently, before being completely abandoned, it served as a junkyard/auto parts store.

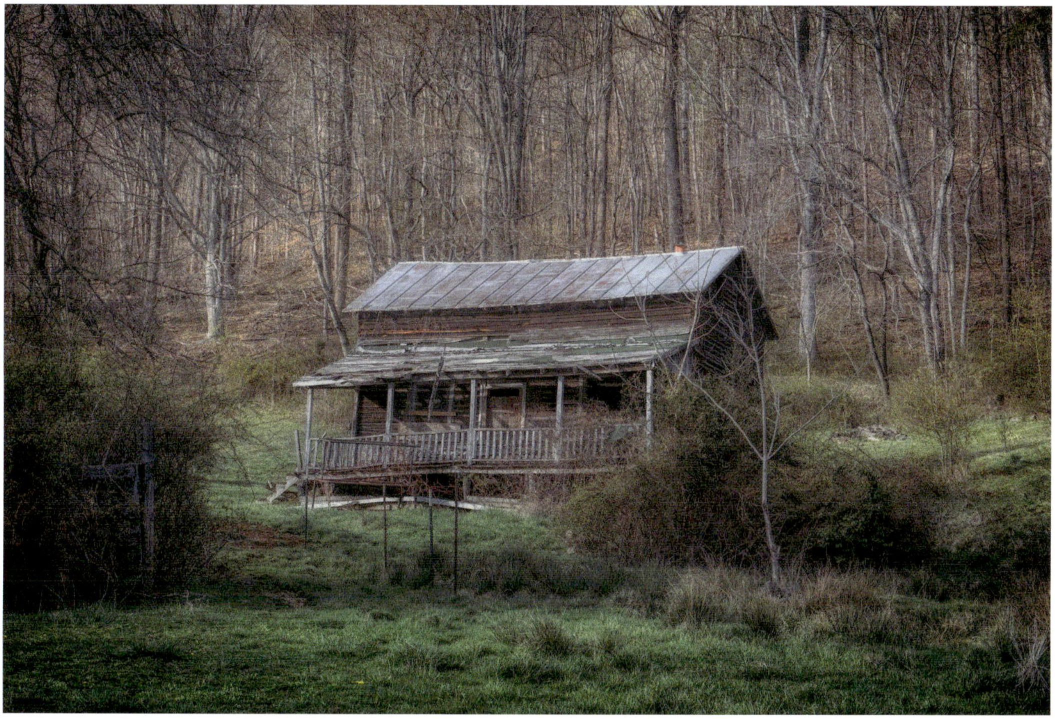

Photo 69: Mountainside Cabin: An old cabin on Route 33 as you cross over the mountain heading towards the town of Elkton. As of the December 2023 Google Street View photo, the front porch has collapsed.

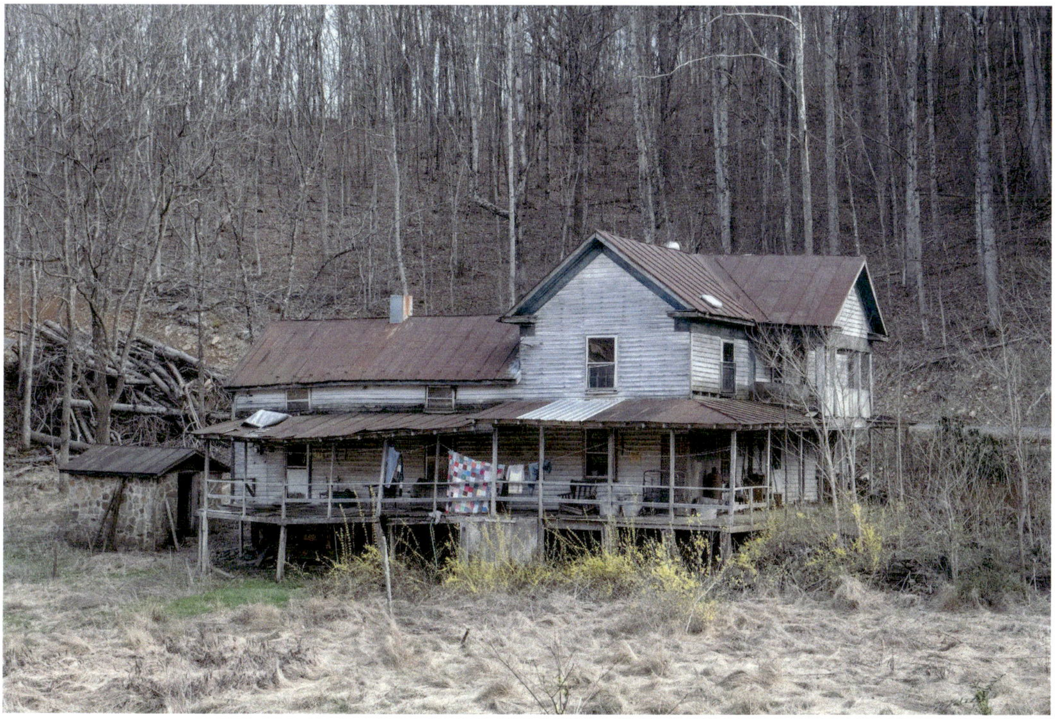

Photo 70: The Laundry House: The infamous laundry house located just down the road from the cabin in Photo 69.

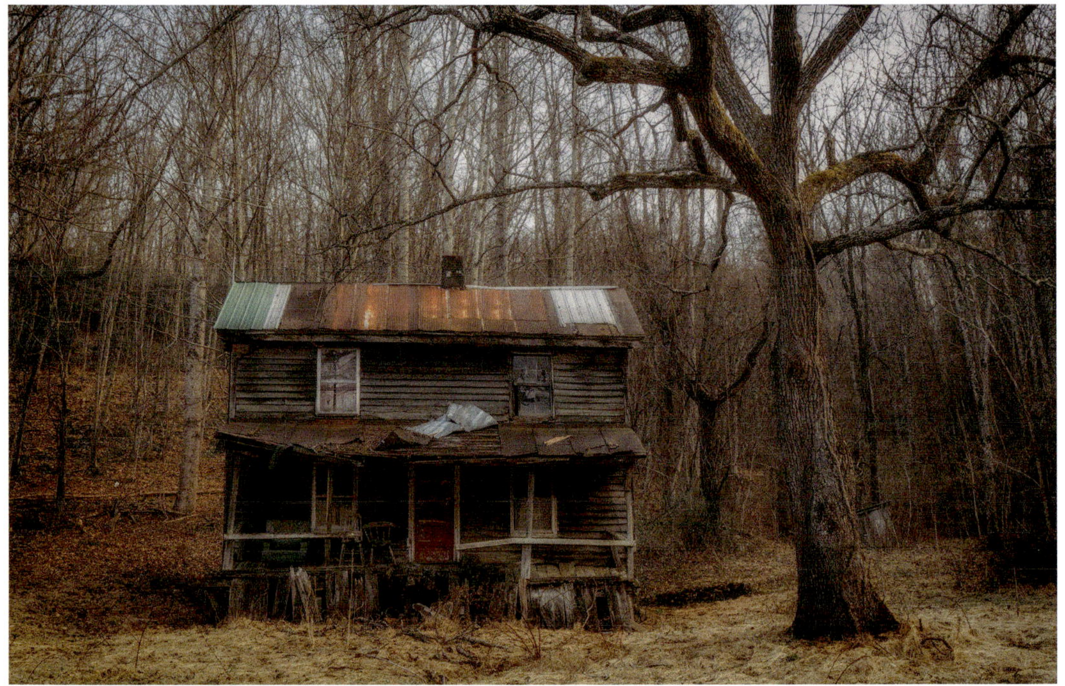

Photo 71: Tʜᴇ Oʟᴅ Mᴏᴜɴᴛᴀɪɴ Hᴏᴍᴇ: The rainbow roof house, as it is called by some, that sits next to the laundry house in Photo 70. As of the January 2024 Google Street View photo, it still stands but it looks like the roof of the front porch is beginning to sag some more. I have a framed print of this photo hanging in my office at work.

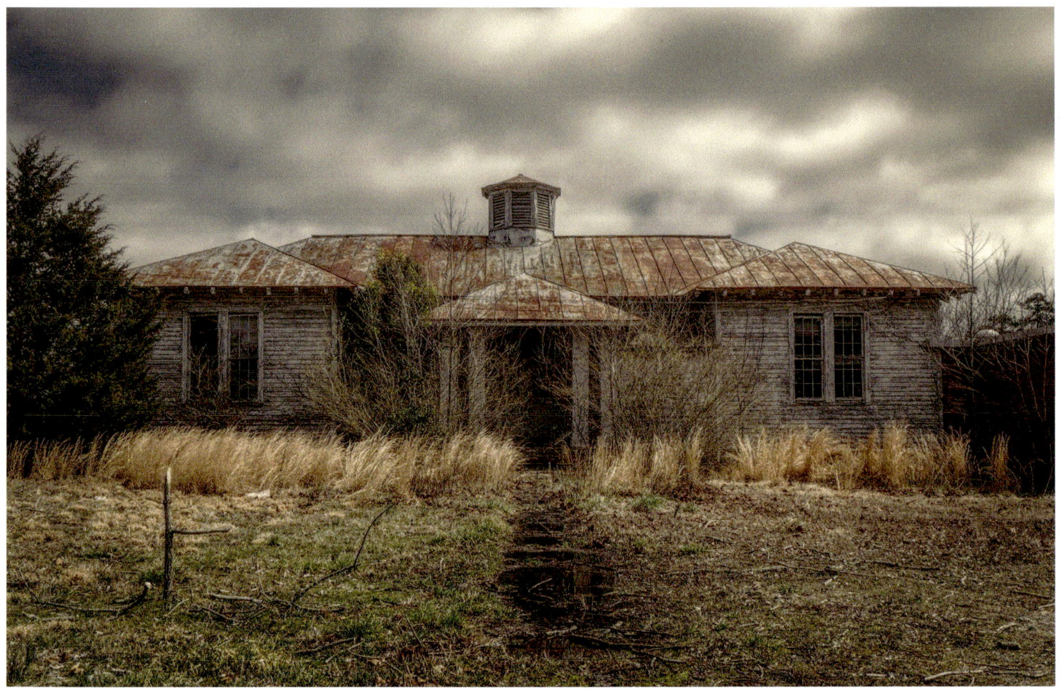

Photo 72: Oʟᴅ Sᴄʜᴏᴏʟ: The old Buckhorn School near Union Level. While this school does still stand, the newer brick portion that can be partially seen on the right side of the photo has since been torn down.

2

SAINT FRANCIS DE SALES SCHOOL FOR GIRLS

In the first volume of *Forgotten Virginia*, I spoke of an area photographer who had made it possible for myself and other photographers to be able to visit and take photographs of the Presidents Heads without us having to trespass to do so. Well, since that time he has teamed up with another area photographer to offer photographic excursions, as well as regular tours, at several different historic locations around the state. That photographer's name is John Plashal, and he, along with the other photographer Fred Schneider, made it possible for me and many others to visit and photograph these next four locations that are detailed in this and the following three chapters.

This first location is the former Saint Francis de Sales School for Girls, which is pictured in Photo 73.

In 1895, a Catholic nun named Katherine Drexel (who was posthumously given sainthood by the Catholic Church) had inherited her family's fortune and decided to buy a large tract of land, which once was the site of the Belmead plantation, and founded two schools dedicated to the education of Native and African American girls and African American boys. Opening in 1896, the Saint Francis School operated for more than seventy years until it finally closed its doors in 1970. During that time, some 5,000 students attended and graduated from this school. The "young ladies," as they prefer to be called, who attended this school were taught to a very high standard of education. Fortunately for us, some of the former students are still with us. To hear them speak of this school is to hear someone speak with pride and gratitude for a place they loved and cherished; a place that gave them the necessary knowledge to go out into the world and become successful; a place that taught them that they could accomplish anything they imagined, no matter their racial origins or social status at the time.

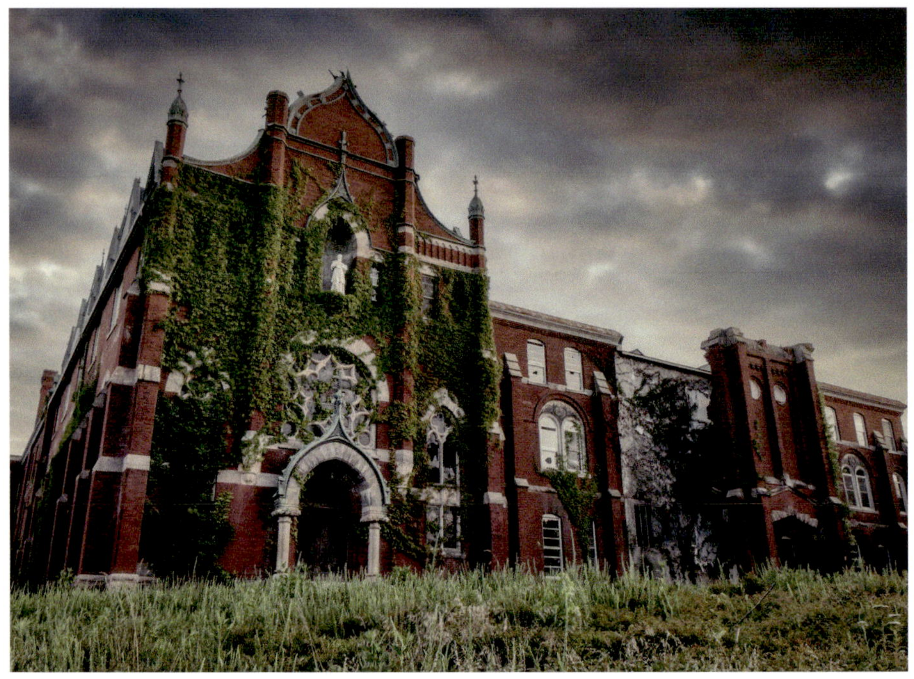

Photo 73: NEGLECTED MONUMENT OF A BYGONE ERA: The front façade of the Saint Francis de Sales School for Girls.

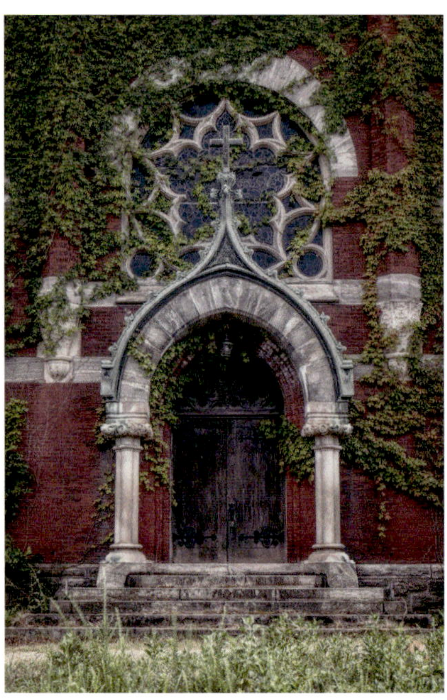

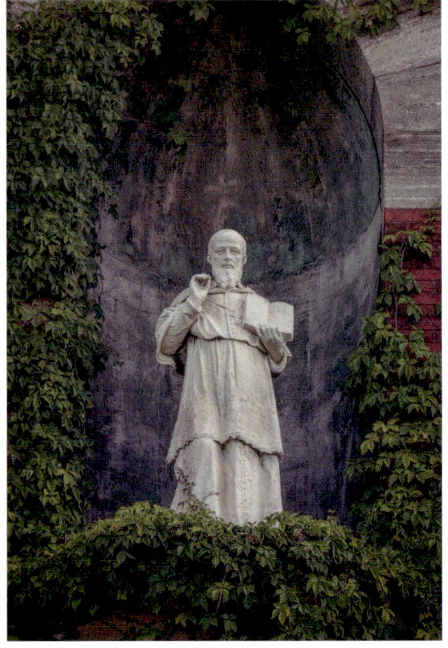

Above left: Photo 74: ABANDONED CHAPEL ENTRANCE: A close-up of the main double doors that lead into the chapel in the Saint Francis School.

Above right: Photo 75: ST. FRANCIS DE SALES: A close-up shot of the statue of Saint Francis de Sales that sits above the entrance to the chapel.

Unfortunately, the main school building is now condemned. This meant that we photographers who were on site that day were not allowed to venture inside the school to capture what I am sure would have been various poignant images of the interiors of this magnificent structure. We were allowed, however, to stand in the doorway and take some photos of the now derelict chapel where many a mass was once held. Photo 76 is the shot I captured of the chapel. Photo 77 shows some of the stained-glass windows in the old chapel that are still intact. Photo 78 is a shot of one of the chapel windows photographed from the outside.

Photo 79 shows a bridge that was crossed over by carriages carrying the newly incoming students onto the property having just been brought in by boat on the James River. From the river, the students could see the Saint Francis school building and the castle-like main building of Saint Emma's Military Academy nearly a mile to the west on the adjacent piece of property.

As one might suspect, there were a lot of people during this time period who were not very happy about these two schools having been established there in rural Virginia. The KKK even once rode in on horses in an attempt to intimidate and frighten the nuns and students at the Saint Francis School. With strength

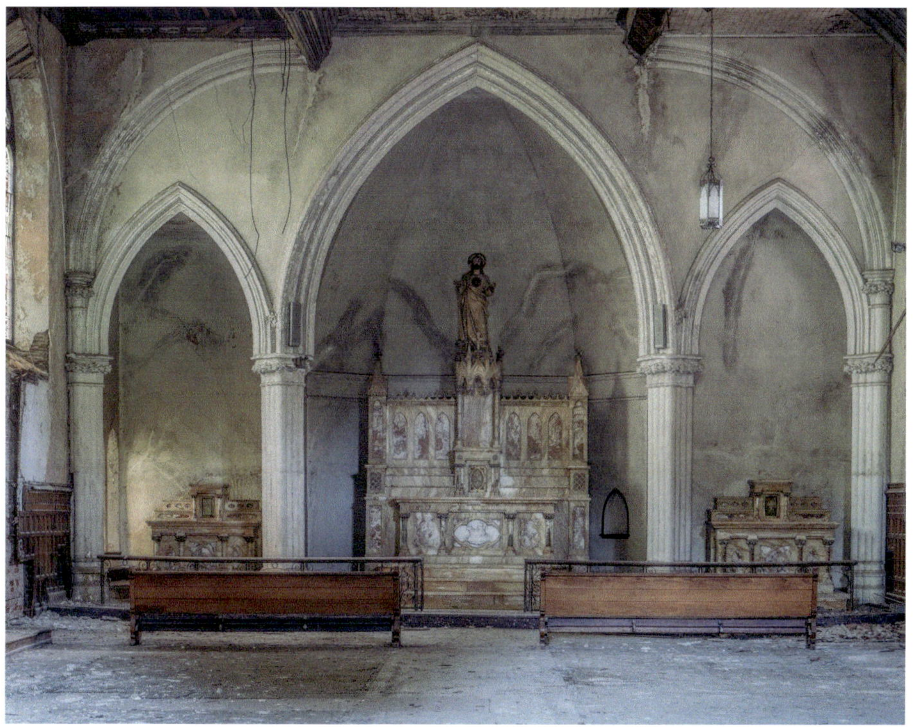

Photo 76: THE FORGOTTEN CHAPEL: The chapel in the Saint Francis School. The girls who attended this school would come to this chapel, at a minimum, on Fridays and Sundays to attend Mass.

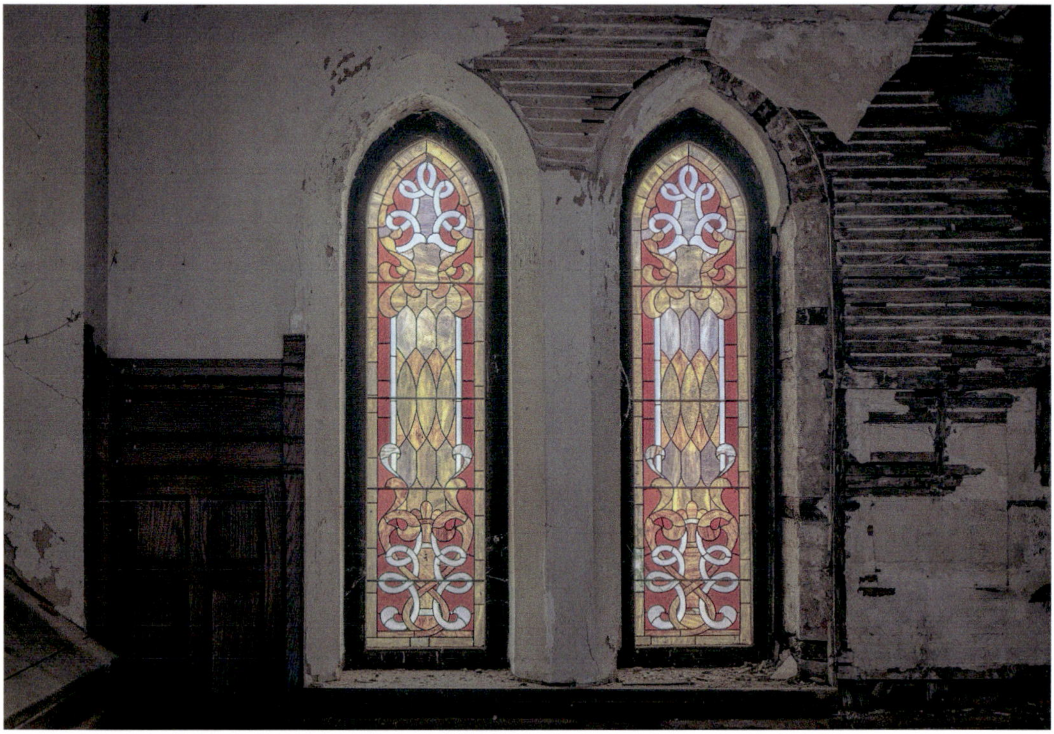

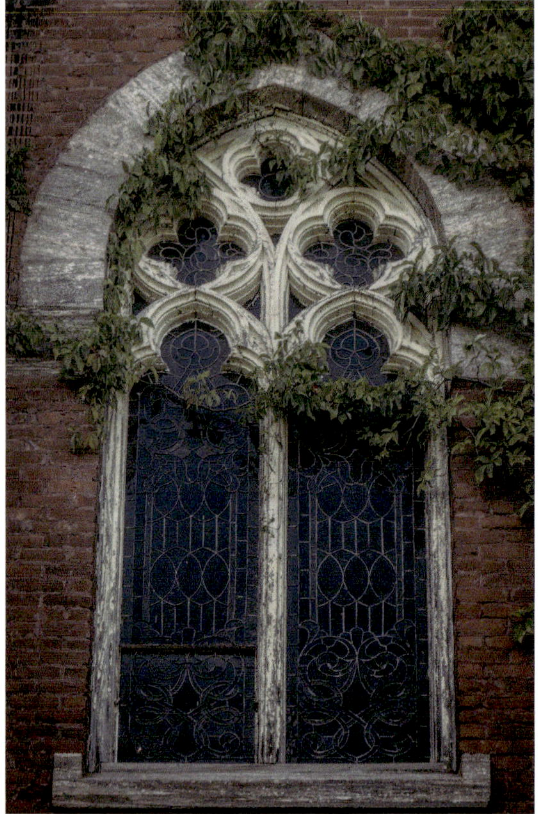

Above: Photo 77: Beauty Amidst the Decay: Some of the stained-glass windows in the chapel.

Left: Photo 78: A Window of Time: Another chapel window photographed from the outside.

and determination, the brave nuns stood their ground standing in the way of the Klansmen. Before long, they were reinforced by the cadets from Saint Emma's who arrived with rifles in hand causing the KKK to retreat. The heroism on display that night by the nuns and the students of both schools is the kind that should be captured in time and heralded over and over again in recorded history or by way of an award-winning cinematic masterpiece.

Photos 80–85 were also taken on the Saint Francis School property.

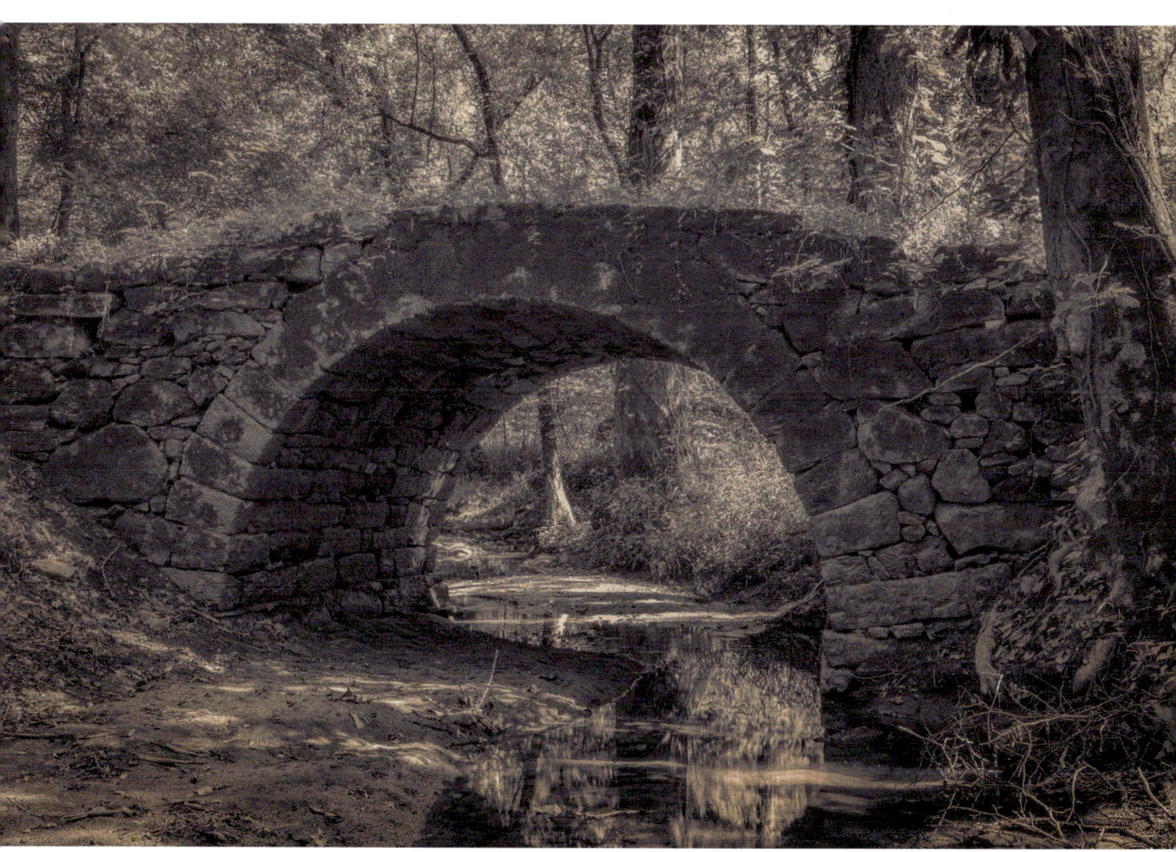

Photo 79: THE ABANDONED CROSSING: An old stone bridge spanning the nearby creek. After arriving to the property by boat on the James River, new students were loaded into a carriage and crossed over this bridge on their way to the school.

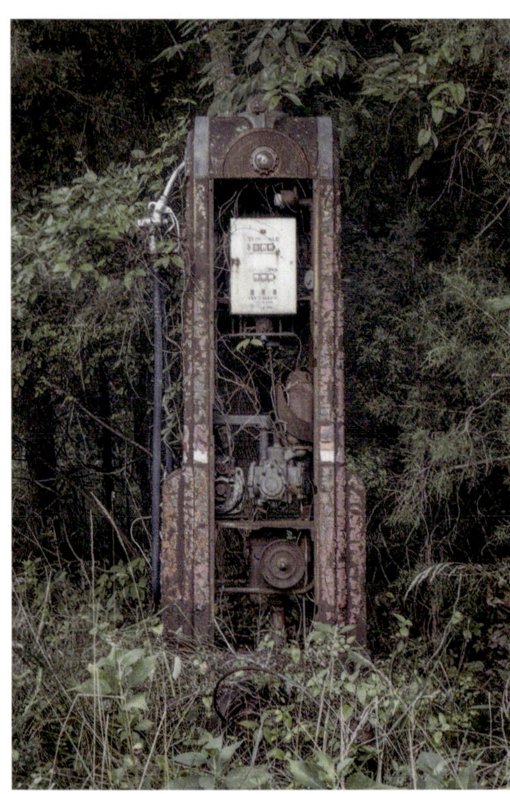

Left: Photo 80: No Sale: An old gas pump that sits along the old road that leads to the bridge in Photo 79.

Below: Photo 81: Final Resting Place of the Nuns: The title says it all. A small graveyard onsite where nuns would be buried when they passed away.

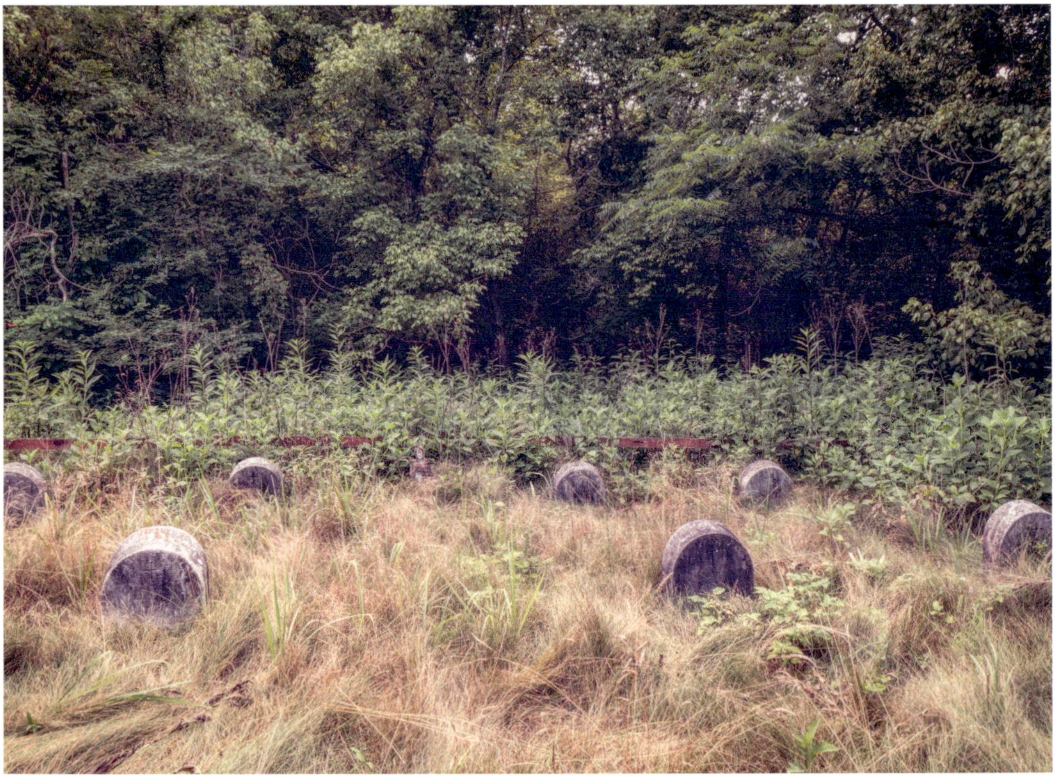

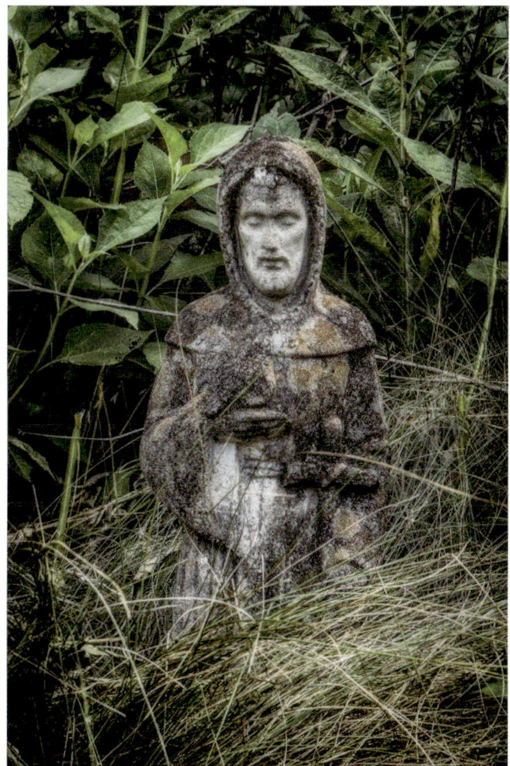

Right: Photo 82: KEEPING WATCH: A small statue watches over the graves of the nuns in the small graveyard. If you look closely, you can see this statue near the center of Photo 81.

Below: Photo 83: THE CHILDREN'S GRAVEYARD: Located near the nuns' graveyard is this small final resting place for students who unfortunately passed away while attending the school.

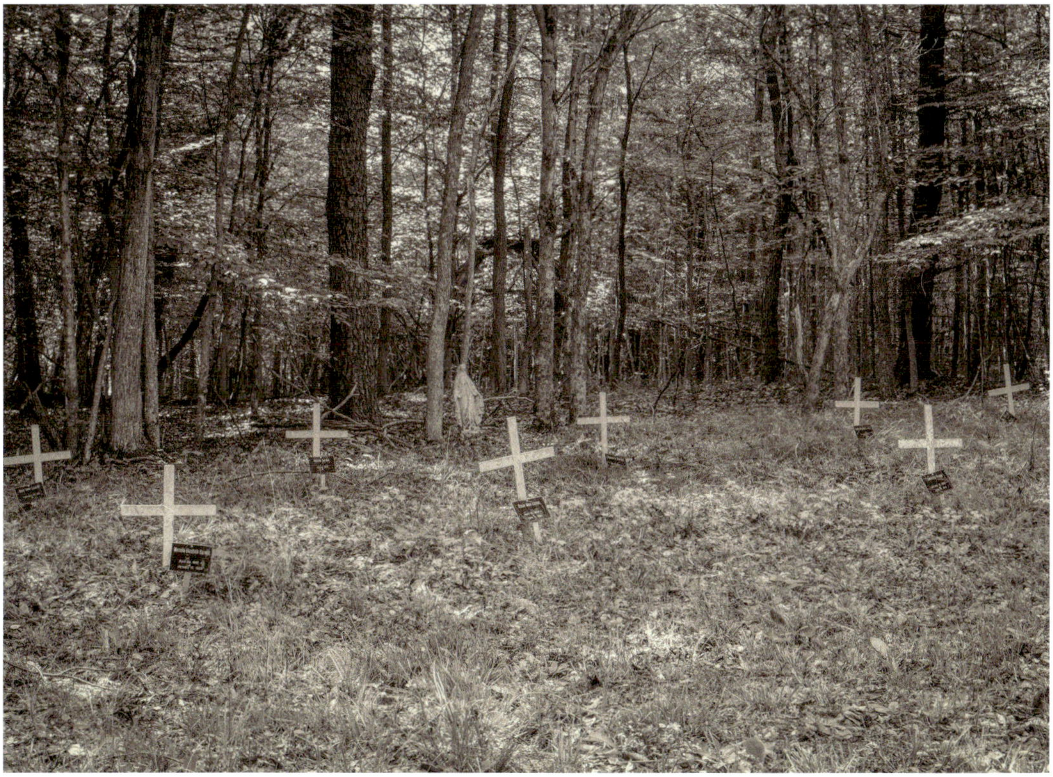

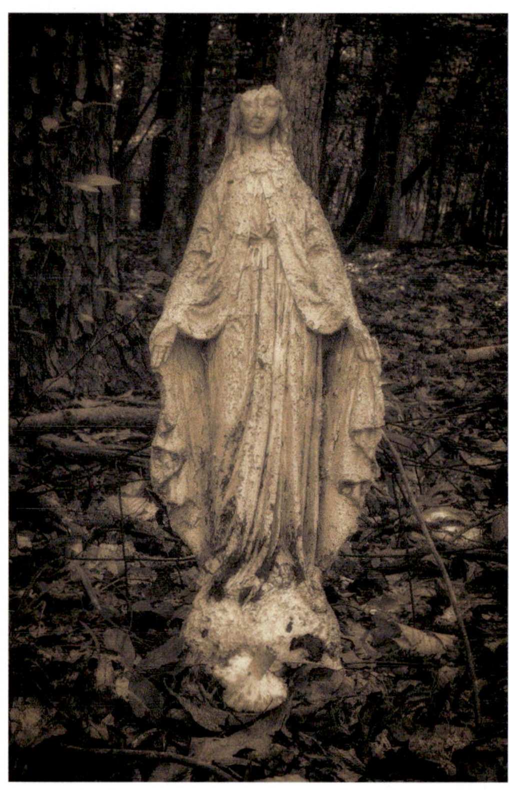

Photo 84: FORGOTTEN MARY: This small statue of the Virgin Mary watches over the graves in the children's graveyard. You can see her near the center of Photo 83.

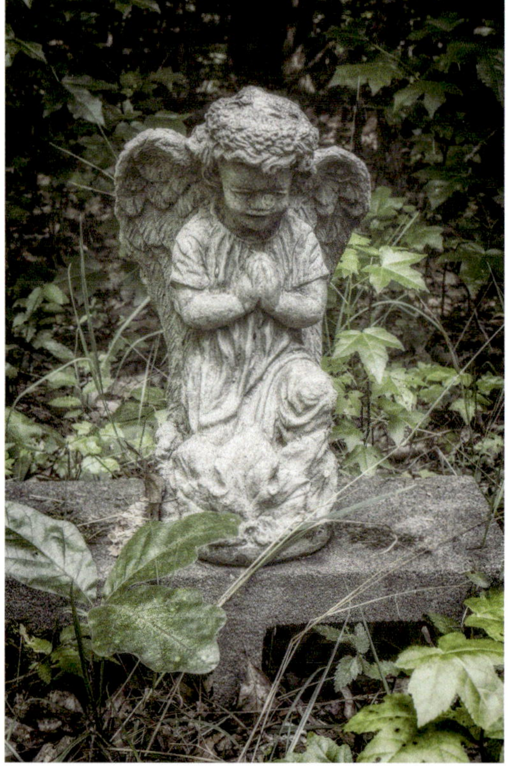

Photo 85: NOW I LAY ME DOWN TO SLEEP: This small statue sits off to the side of the children's graveyard as though this angel is praying for the girls who are buried there. If you look very closely, you will see that someone, at some time, put a little smiley face sticker on the statue's nose.

3

SAINT EMMA'S MILITARY ACADEMY

In 1899, the other school that was located just to the west of Saint Francis School opened: Saint Emma's Military Academy. This school has the distinct honor of being the only military academy dedicated for the education of African American young men in the country. By its closure in 1972 more than 10,000 students were educated at and graduated from Saint Emma's. Upon graduating, the cadets would not only receive academic diplomas, but trade and military diplomas as well. Throughout its operating history, there were many buildings built on the campus by the students as part of their vocational training. Unfortunately, none of these buildings are left standing. The only building still standing is the one that the students referred to as "the big house." This was the main plantation house from the years prior to the founding of the school and is pictured in Photo 86.

Much like that which was taking place at the Saint Francis School, the cadets who were enrolled at this academy received a very high standard of education. They were also grouped into military-style regiments and underwent military training there on the grounds while wearing their uniforms. And just like Saint Francis, the graduates of this school who are still with us speak lovingly and reverently about this academy.

Both schools have been featured in local news stories on multiple news stations and Saint Emma's was even featured on the nationally televised program *CBS Saturday Morning*. Through the proceeds generated from the tours, John Plashal, Fred Schneider, and the property's owner are looking to have historical markers placed for both of the schools and perhaps even have a museum created in honor of the schools.

On a piece of property where a small cemetery still exists that holds the final resting places of more than 100 individuals who were formerly enslaved there, it

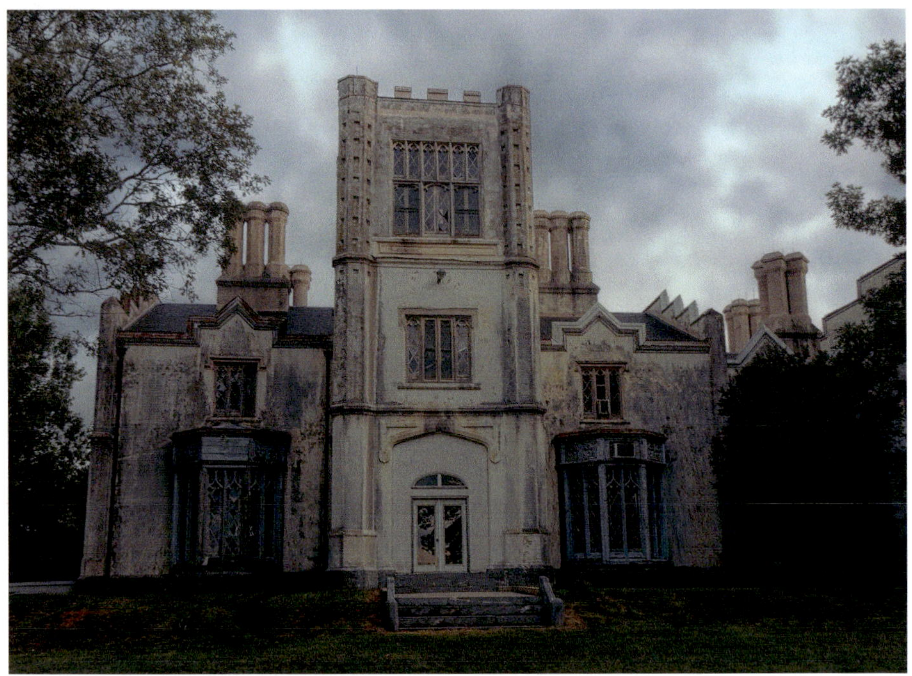

Photo 86: Sᴛ. Eᴍᴍᴀ's: The "big house" at Saint Emma's Military Academy. This building also was the main plantation house on the Belmead Plantation before the establishment of the two schools.

is quite the lasting legacy that thousands of African and Native American young men and women received quality educations and became empowered to become more than society, at the time, would have them be; a legacy that indeed should be remembered and honored.

Photos 87–105 were all taken on Saint Emma's property.

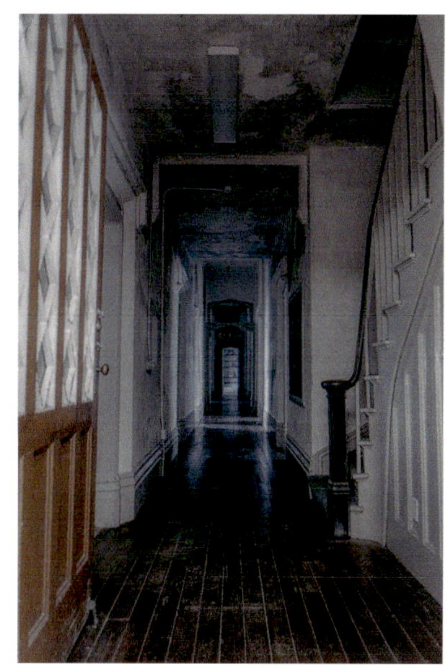 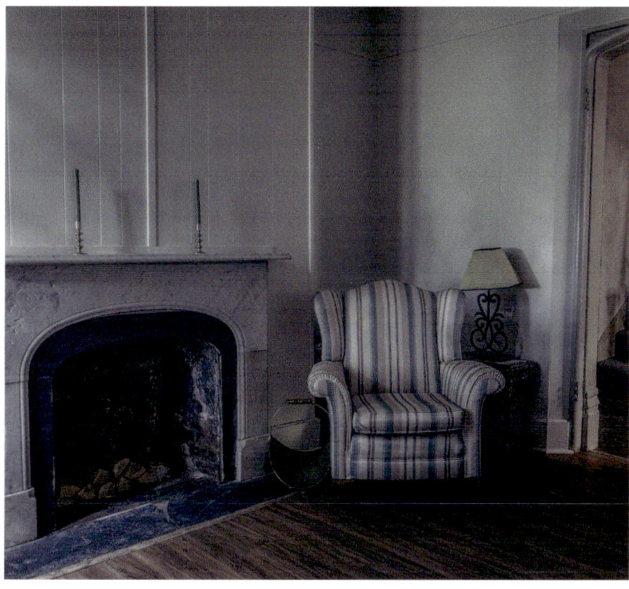

Above left: Photo 87: The Hall of Forgotten Footsteps: The main hallway on the first floor of the "big house."

Above right: Photo 88: The Old Sitting Room: A small parlor on the first floor of the main Saint Emma's building.

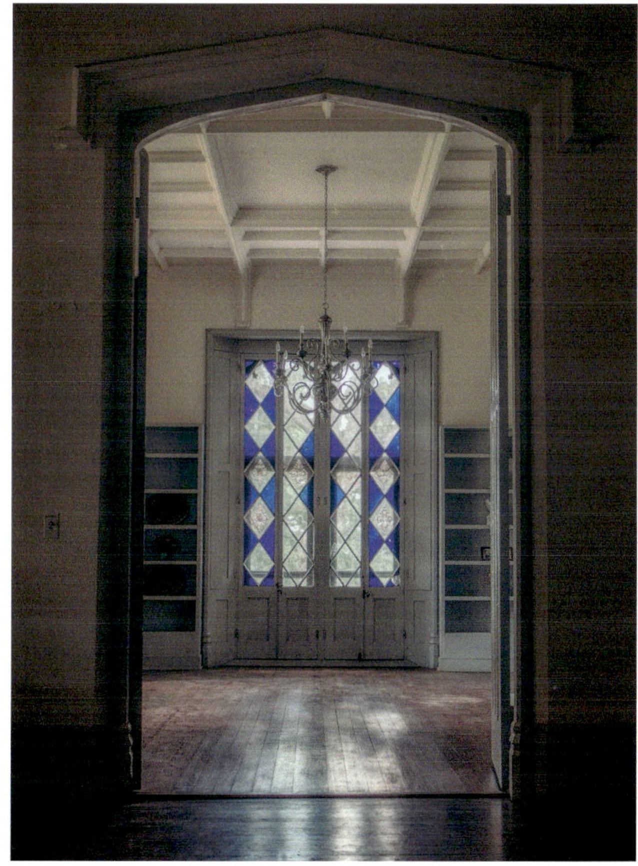

Photo 89: Through the Doorway: Looking from one room to the next in the main building.

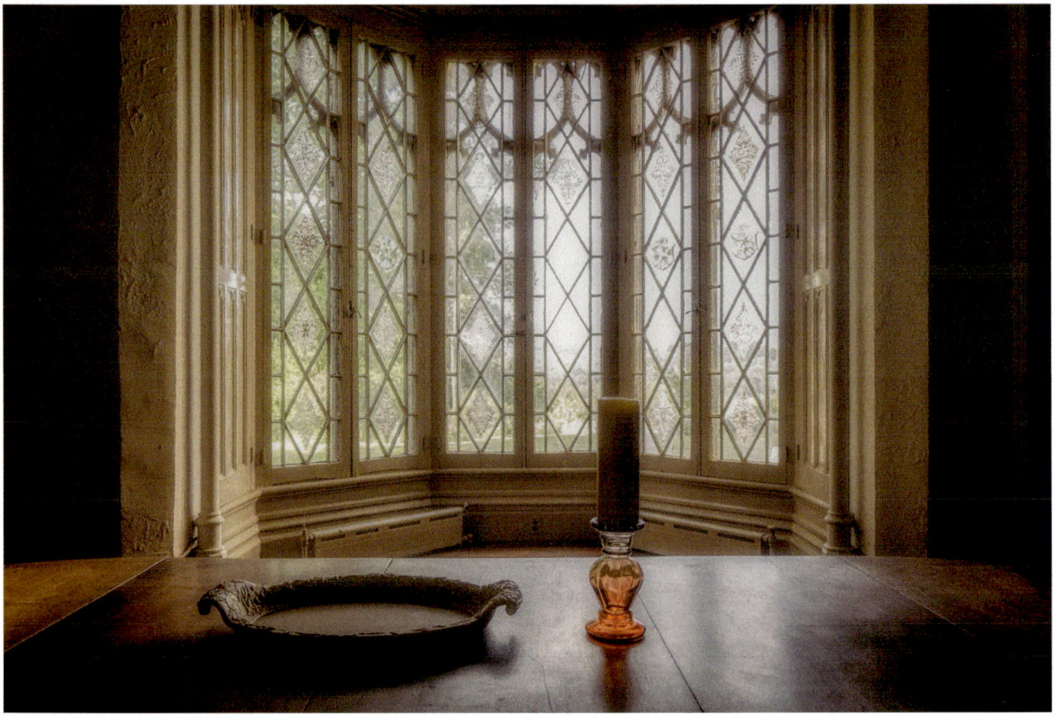

Photo 90: AT THE EMPTY TABLE: A photo taken in the same spot as Photo 89 but looking to the side of the room. This room appeared as though it were a dining room at one time.

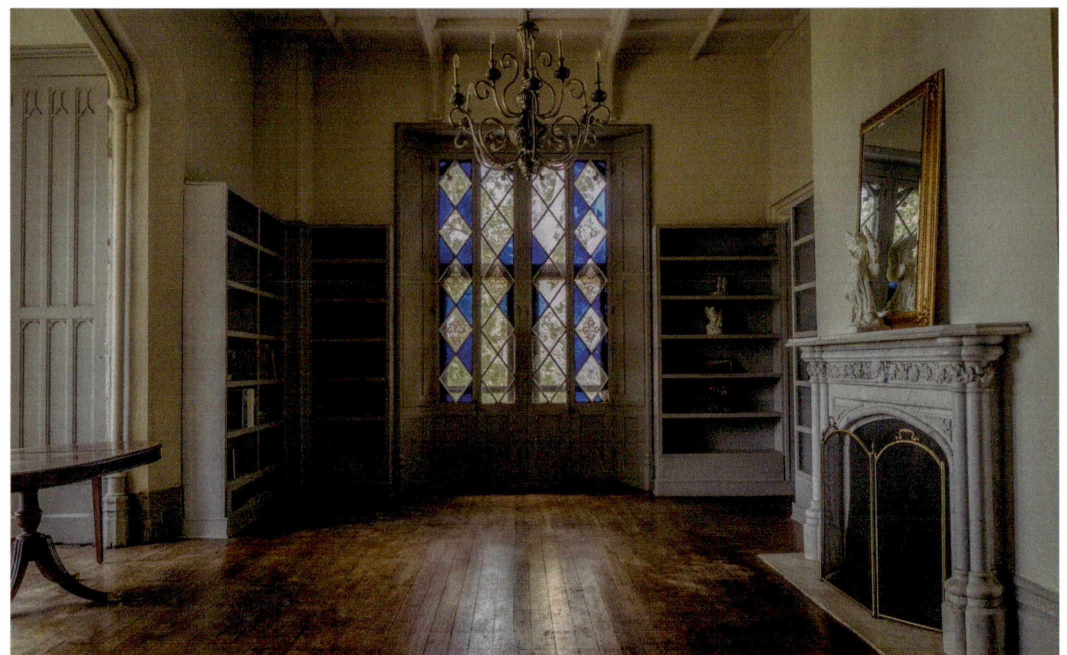

Photo 91: THE HEARTHSIDE STUDY: This is the same window as shown in Photo 89. That particular window still has the names of some of the students who attended the academy etched into the clear panes of glass. I attempted to capture some on camera, but it unfortunately could not focus on them.

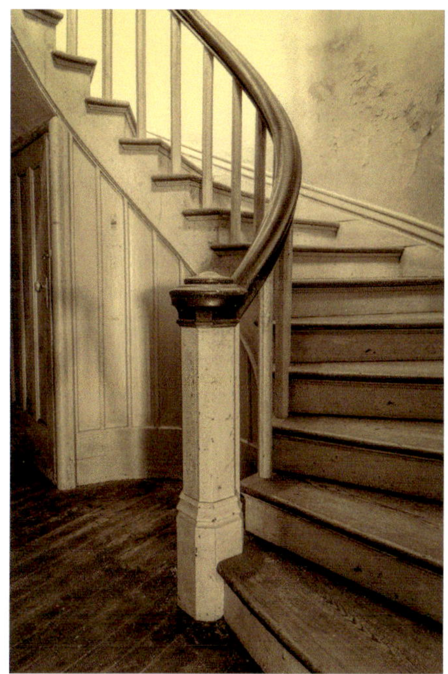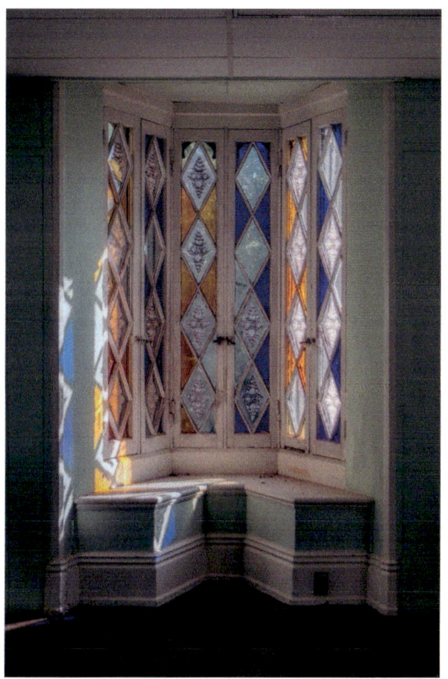

Above left: Photo 92: THE CREAKY STAIRS: The main staircase that goes up to the second floor in the main building.

Above right: Photo 93: SECOND-FLOOR WINDOW: A window in what looked to be a bedroom on the second floor of the main building.

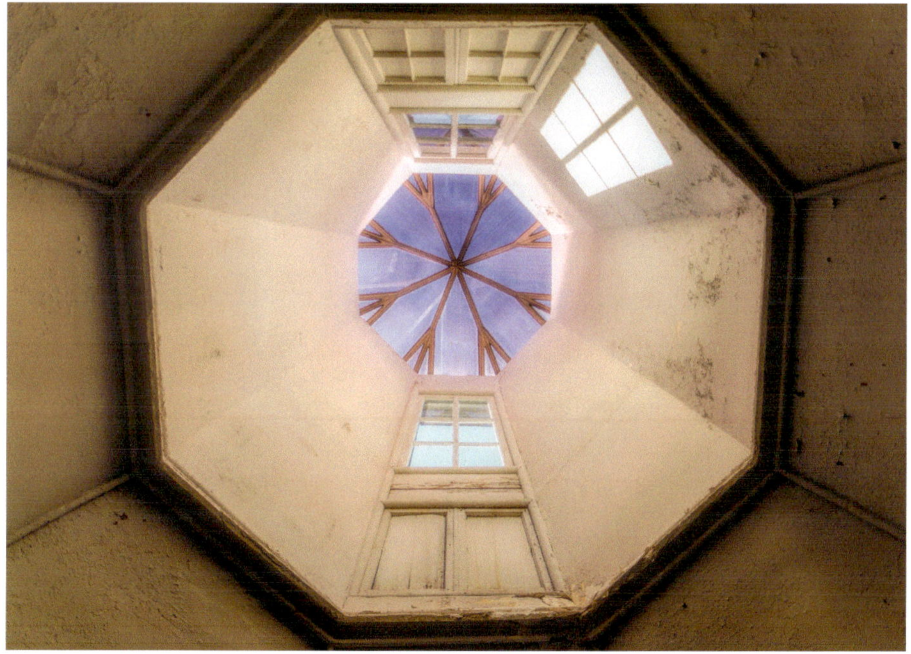

Photo 94: 1:30: Standing in (or near, I cannot remember which) the bedroom in Photo 93, I looked up and saw this sight. I thought it looked really cool, so I took a photo. The sun shining onto the sidewall in the upper right part of the photo reminds me of an analog clock reading 1:30.

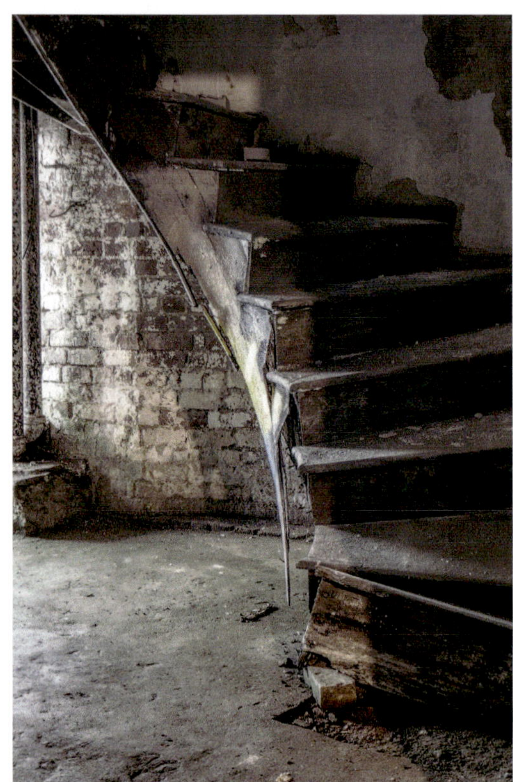

Left: Photo 95: THE FORGOTTEN STAIRCASE: This staircase is in the basement of the main building and is directly beneath the staircase shown in Photo 92. I think it is pretty safe to say that it is not safe to use these stairs!

Below: Photo 96: THE DUNGEON PRISON CELL: This is not really a prison cell. Sometimes I name photos based on what my imagination sees in them, which is the case in this instance. I am not sure what this is other than a side room in the basement with a dirt floor, but that definitely does not sound as intriguing as a dungeon prison cell!

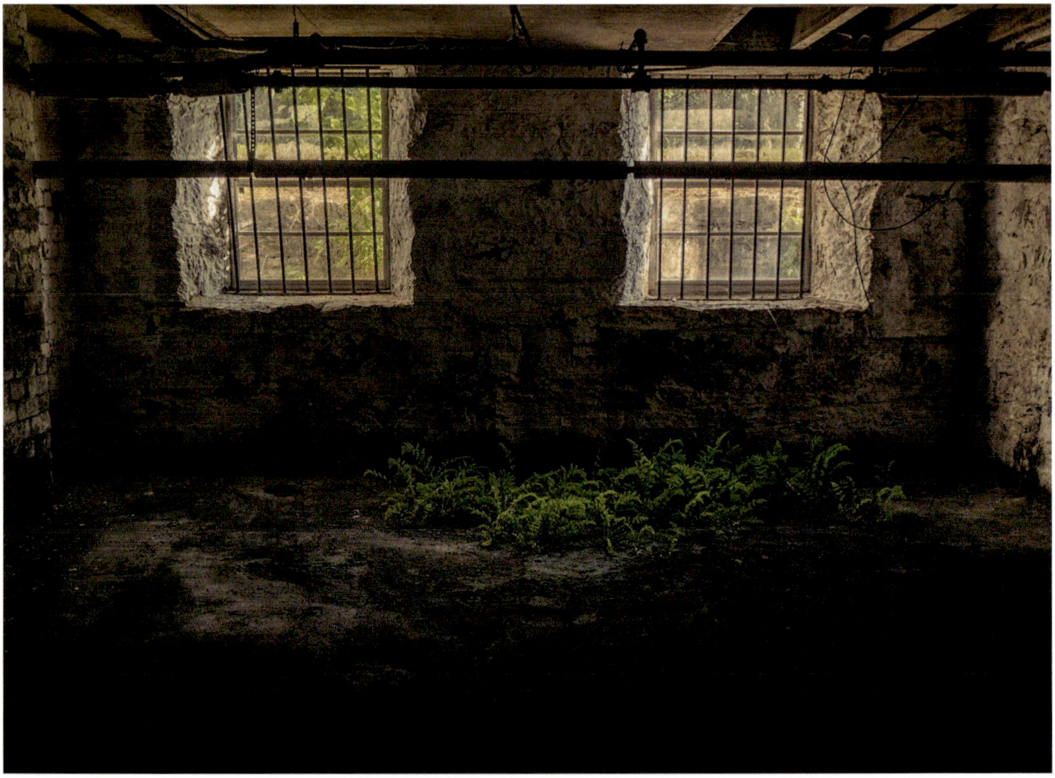

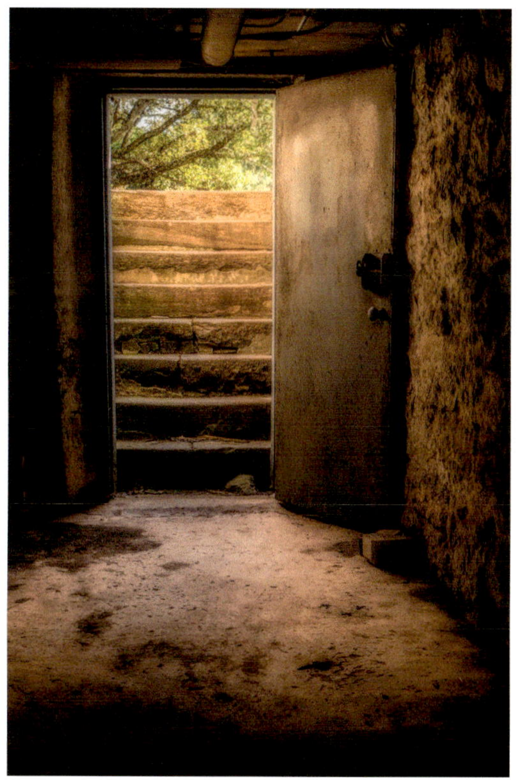

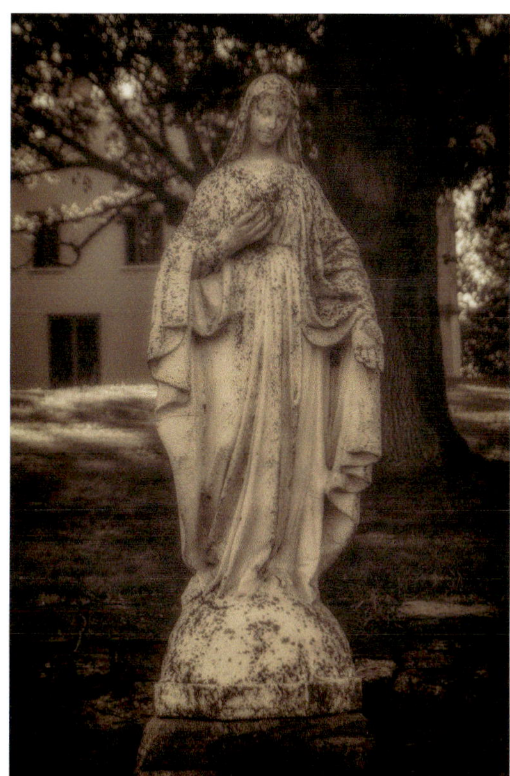

Above left: Photo 97: THE DUNGEON EXIT: Continuing with my dungeon theme we have this photo. This is the exit way to the outside from the basement.

Above right: Photo 98: IMMACULATE HEART OF MARY: That is actually what this statue is called. It stands down the hill from the mansion overlooking visitors as they drive up to the former military campus.

Right: Photo 99: THE CEMETERY ENTRANCE: Hidden away back in the woods, a little more than three-tenths of a mile to the west of the mansion is another little cemetery. I do not know for sure, but I assume this one is for those who attended Saint Emma's.

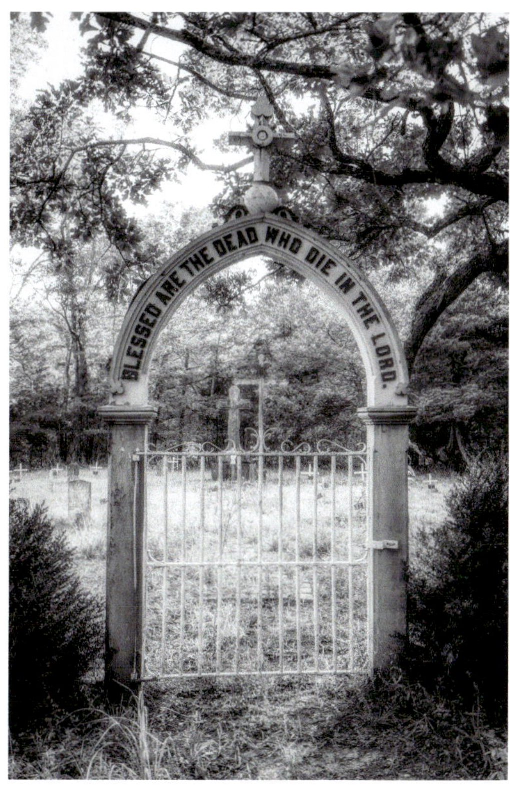

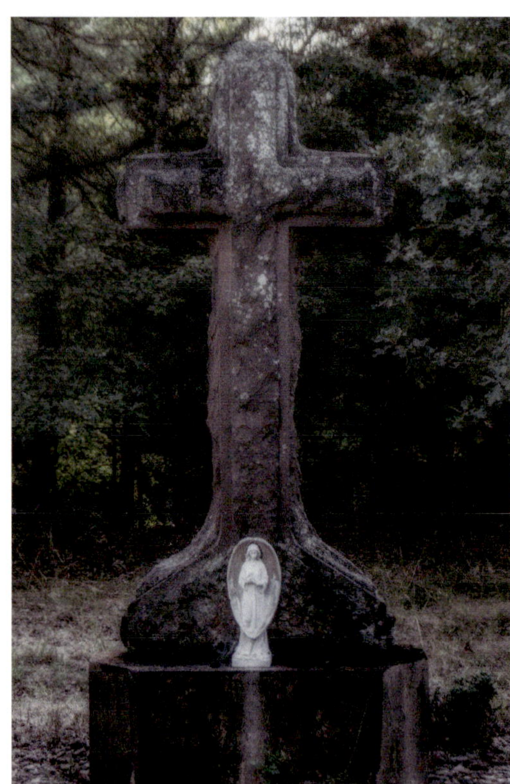

Left: Photo 100: Mary on the Cross: A large cross with a small statue of the Virgin Mary sits near the back of the cemetery in Photo 99.

Below: Photo 101: The Old Witch's Hut: Letting my imagination run wild again, I came up with that name because it sounded a lot better than "The Hog House" which is what this little structure actually is.

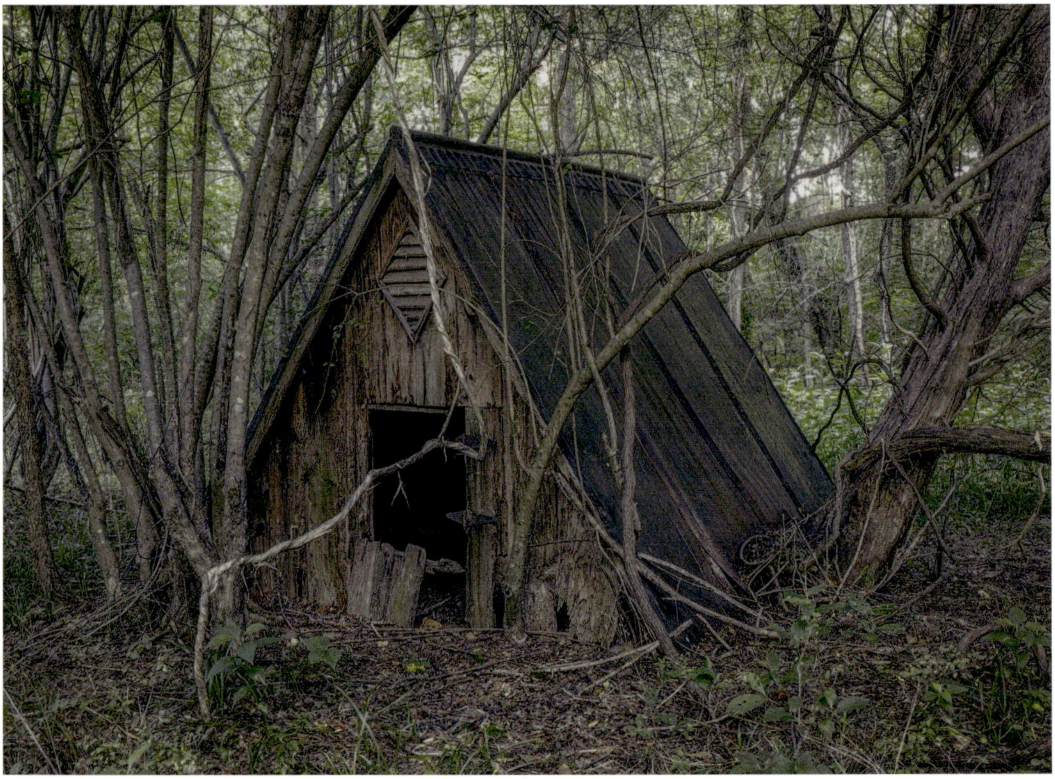

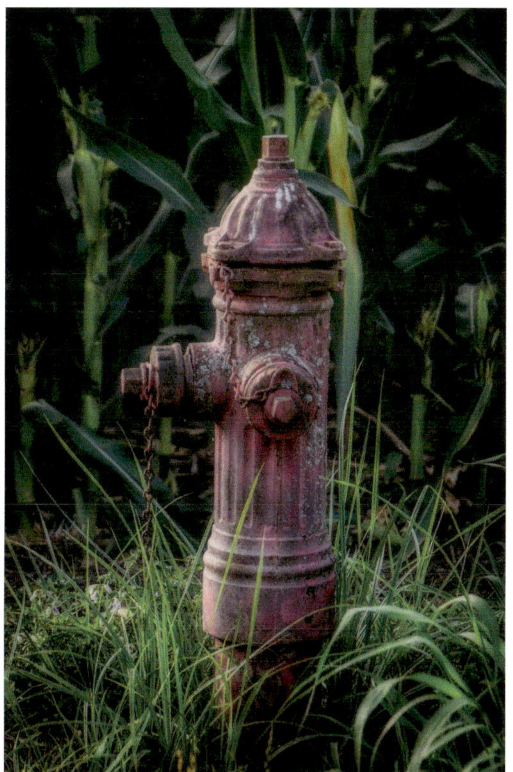

Photo 102: DEHYDRANTED: Do you see what I did there? As I drove around the outskirts of Saint Emma's property, I came across this old fire hydrant at the edge of a cornfield. It looked so old and out of place that I had to get a photo of it.

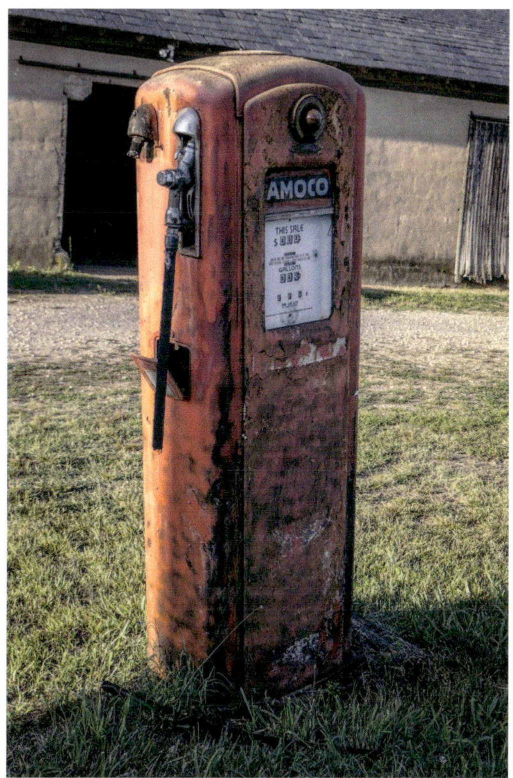

Photo 103: SELF SERVICE: Though not nearly as old as the gas pump in Photo 80, this one still has some age on it. This is one of two old gas pumps next to the old stables on the property.

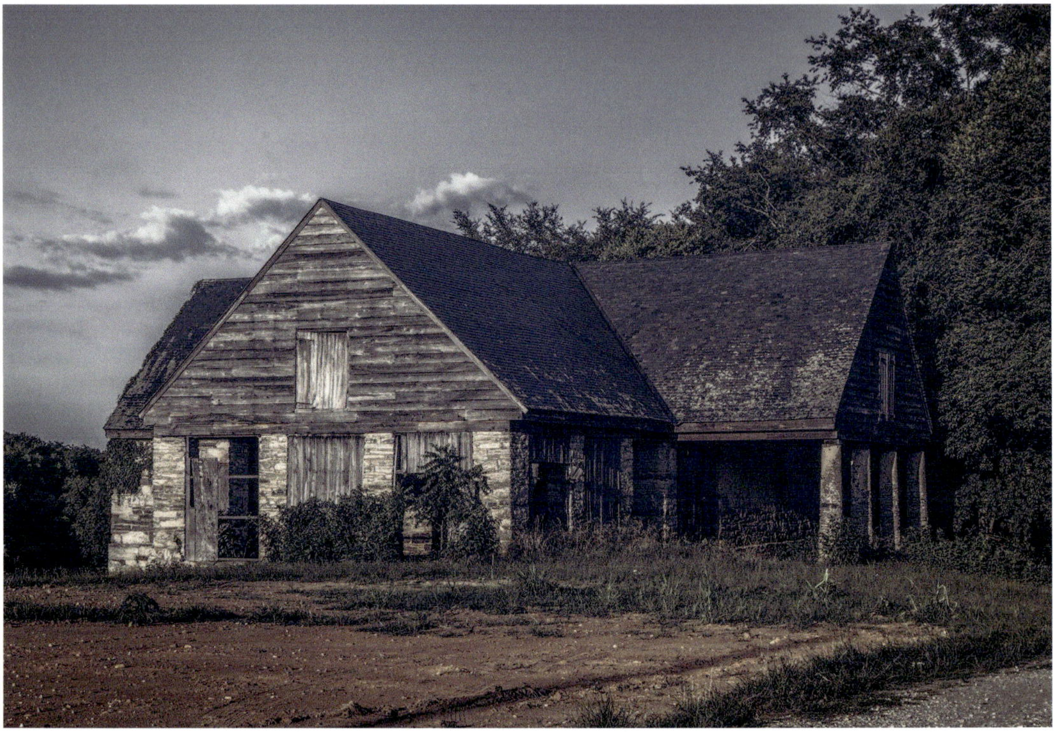

Photo 104: THE OLD GRANARY: This old building served as the granary on the property.

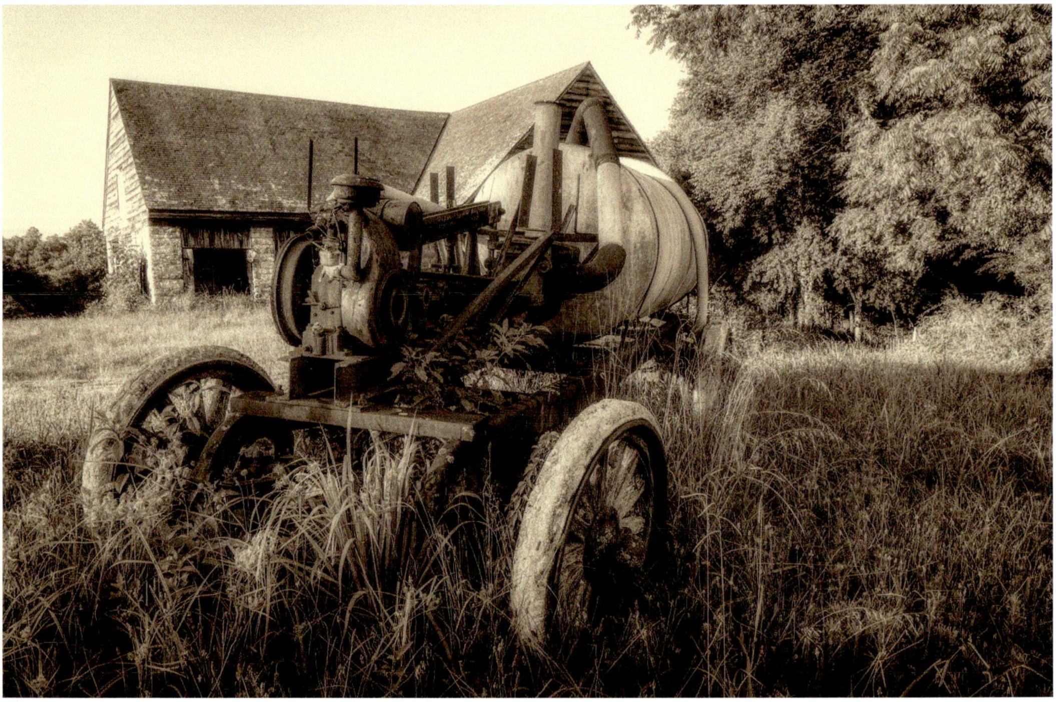

Photo 105: RUSTIC NEGLECT: With the granary from Photo 104 in the background, an old water truck sits neglected as nature tries to reclaim it.

4

SWANNANOA

Anyone who has ever lived in Richmond is familiar with Maymont Park and the story of the former owners of the property. The property was once the home of Major James Dooley and his wife, Sarah "Sallie" Mae Dooley. The mansion in which they lived is still located within the park and can be toured. Major Dooley left the home and property to be donated to the city of Richmond to be used as a park upon the death of his wife. What most people do not know, however, is that the Dooleys had a "summer home." I used quotations there on purpose because it was much more than what you or I would imagine a summer home to be. This was a three-story, 23,000-square-foot palatial estate that contained thirty-six rooms and seven bathrooms located on top of Afton Mountain overlooking both the Rockfish and Shenandoah Valleys. The Dooleys named this estate Swannanoa. It is pictured in Photo 106.

The exterior construction of the mansion was completed in 1913, with work on the interior continuing for another eight years afterwards. The mansion was fully equipped with running water and electricity and even had a telephone system. The electricity was generated by a dedicated electrical plant that was located on the 763-acre property. The mansion also holds the distinction of having the largest Tiffany stained-glass window contained within a home in the United States. Major Dooley had the 4,000-piece window created to depict his wife in her garden there at Swannanoa. The window is located on the landing of the main staircase in the home and is shown in Photo 107.

Unfortunately, because Swannanoa was not completed until the Dooleys were nearing the end of their lives, they only used the home for twelve years. Upon the death of Major Dooley, his wife left the home to his sisters. The sisters soon sold the

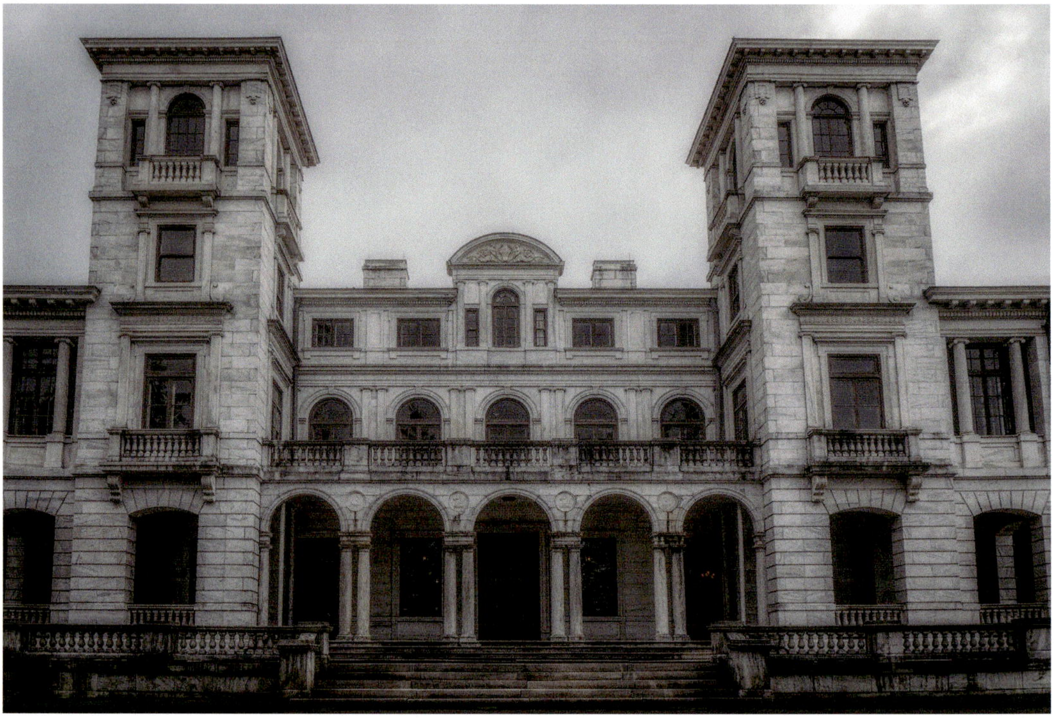

Photo 106: Mountaintop Summer Home: The front façade of the Swannanoa Mansion.

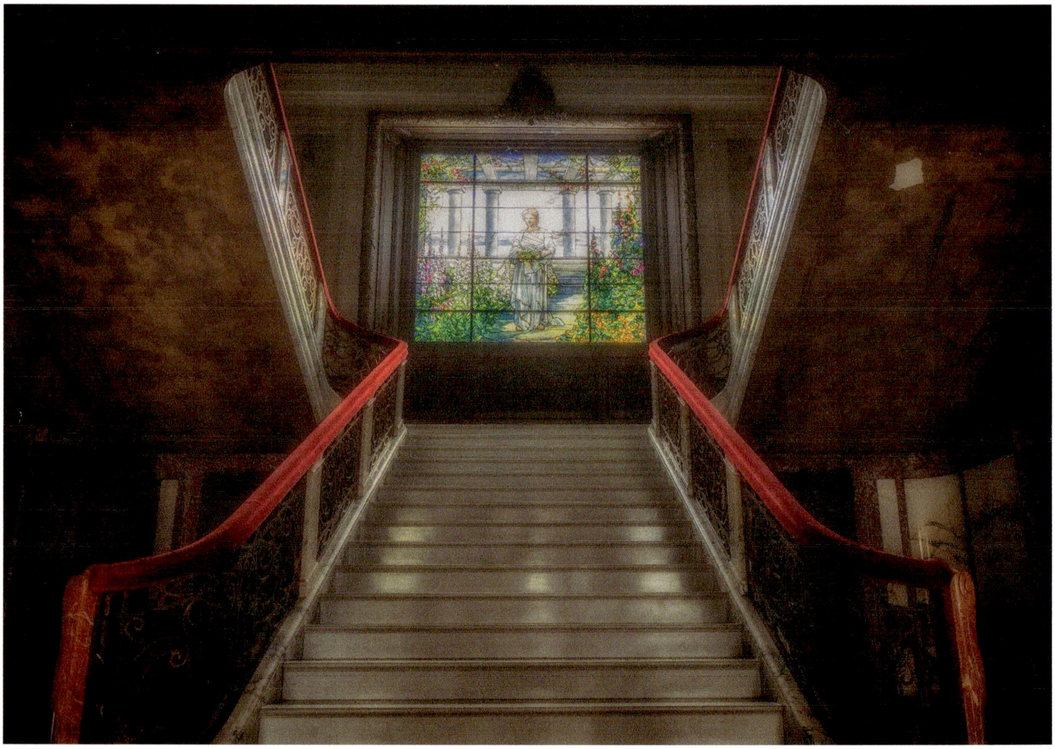

Photo 107: The Tiffany Window: The Tiffany Window depicting Mrs. Dooley on the landing of the main staircase.

property. The new owners then turned it into a country club and golf course. During its time as a country club, President Calvin Coolidge and his wife stayed on the property for Thanksgiving one year. However, due to the hardships caused by the great depression, the owners were forced to sell Swannanoa to avoid bankruptcy. Not long thereafter, Dooley heir, Alice Dooley purchased the estate and unsuccessfully attempted to revive the property as the country club it once was. Over the years the property passed from one owner to another until the current owners, Skyline Swannanoa, Inc. purchased it in 1999 and have operated the estate as a private event venue since 2007. Visitation inquiries can be made by visiting the Swannanoa Facebook page or through their website (skyline-swannanoa-inc.square.site). Photos 108–126 were all taken on the Swannanoa property.

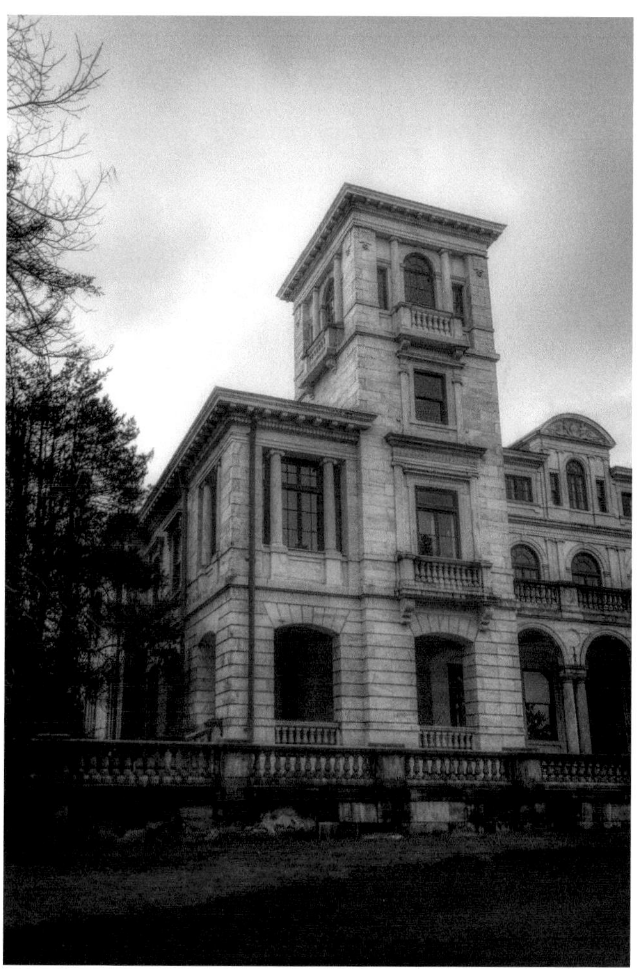

Photo 108: SWANNANOA: A shot of the southeast corner of the mansion.

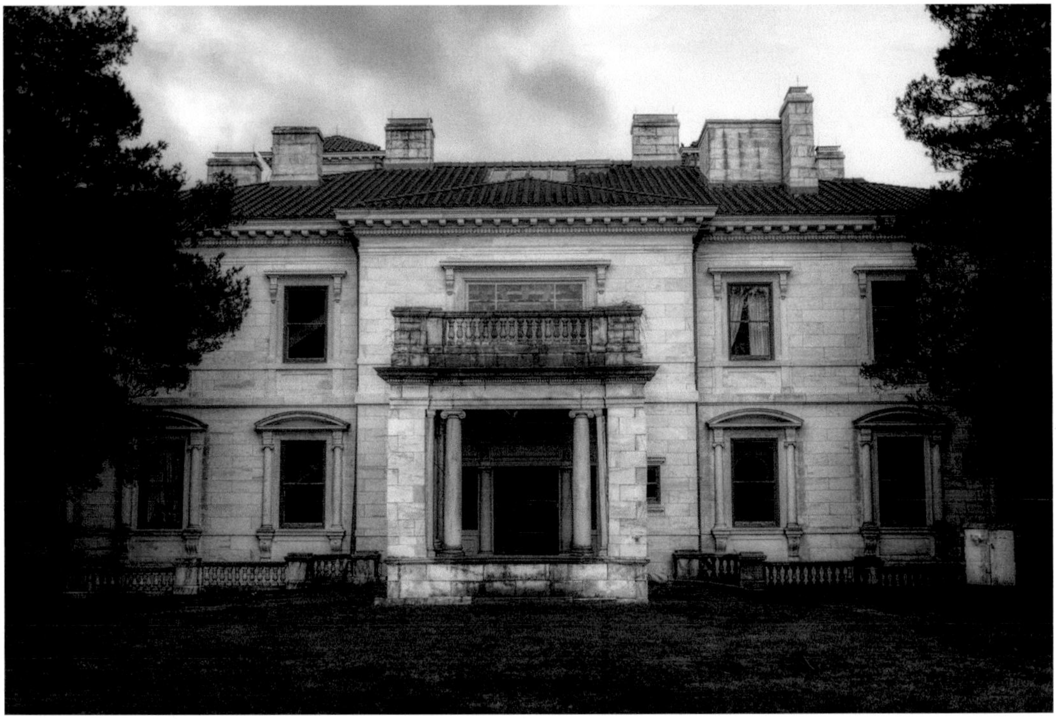

Photo 109: SWANNANOA FROM BEHIND: Not much use of imagination in that title, huh? This is a shot of the rear façade of the mansion.

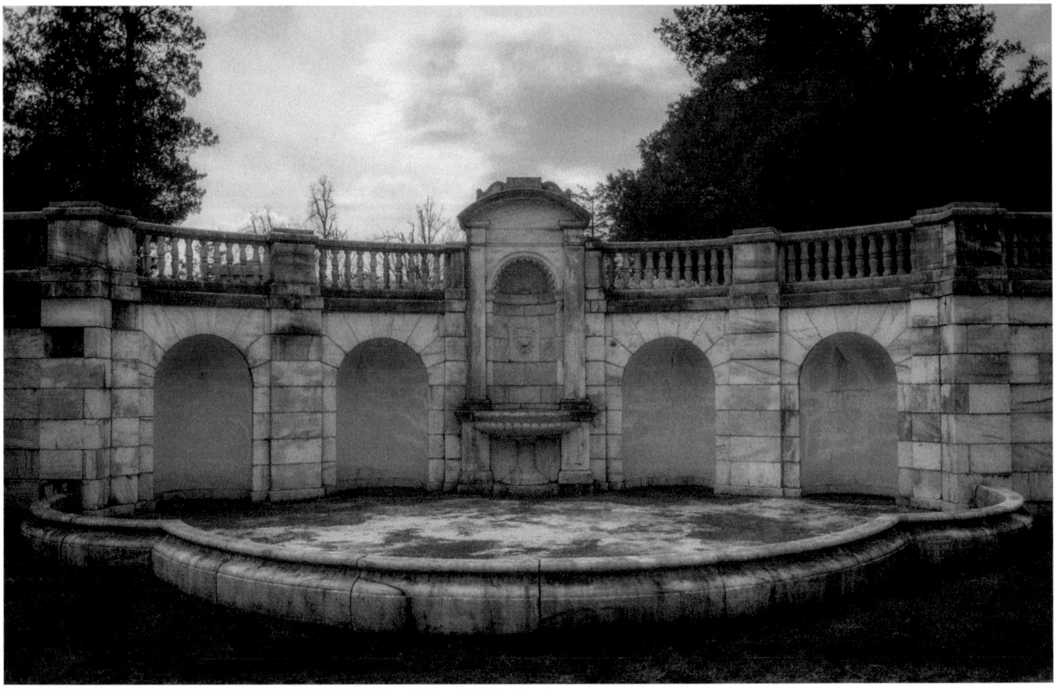

Photo 110: BACKYARD FOUNTAIN: Directly behind the mansion sits this illustrious fountain. It would have been neat to see it back when it was working.

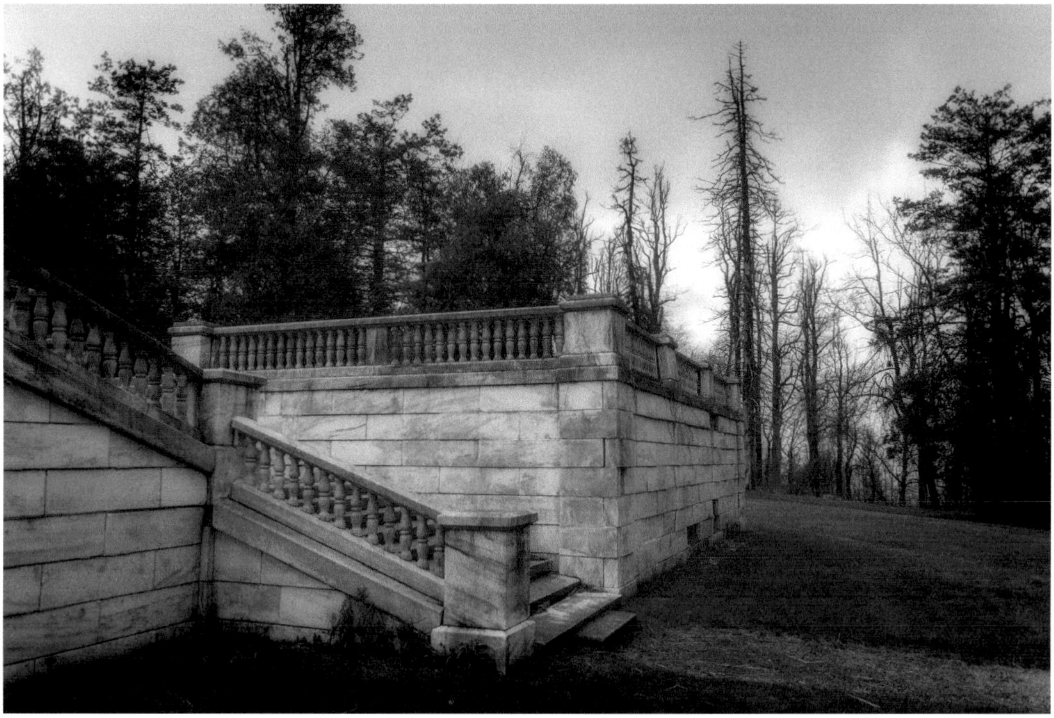

Photo 111: THE MANSION BACKYARD STEPS: This is one set of stairs that leads up above the fountain. 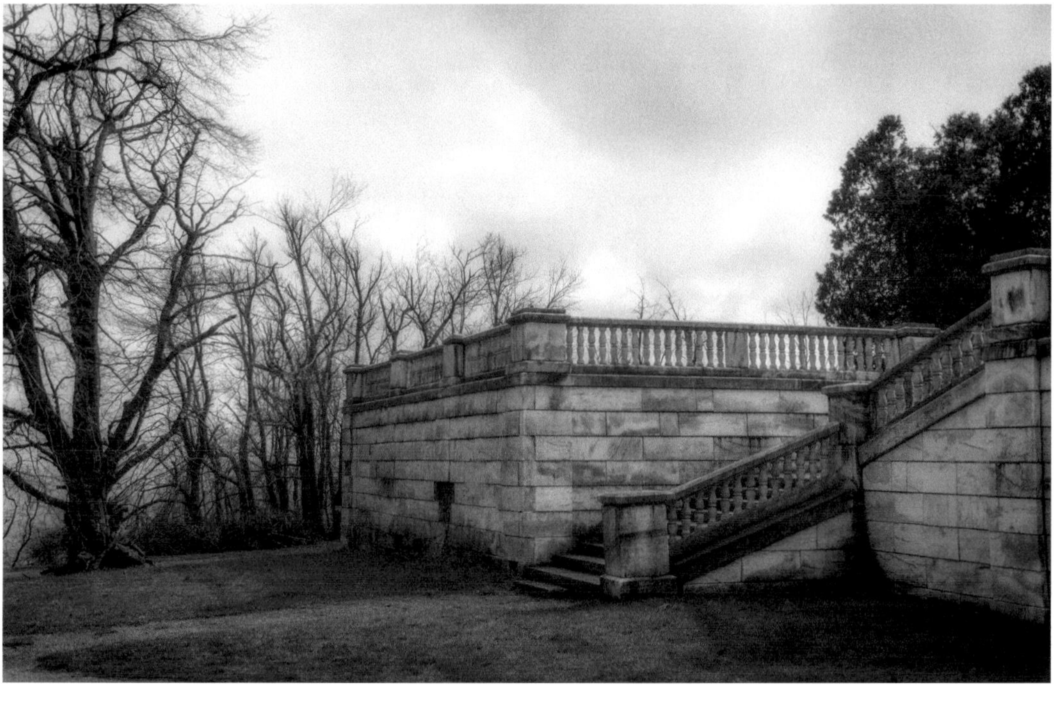
Photo 112: THE MANSION BACKYARD STEPS 2: As you might have guessed from that incredibly clever title, this is the second set of stairs. Each set is located on either side of the fountain.

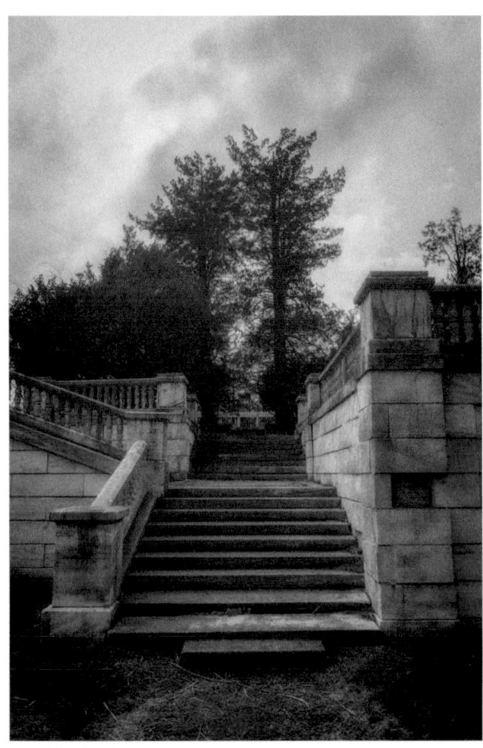

Left: Photo 113: THE MARBLE STAIRS: Just in case you have not seen enough details in these two staircases, here is a straight-on shot of the one from Photo 111.

Below: Photo 114: A BENCH ON WHICH TO REST: At the top of the two staircases, with the rear of the mansion behind it, sits this little bench.

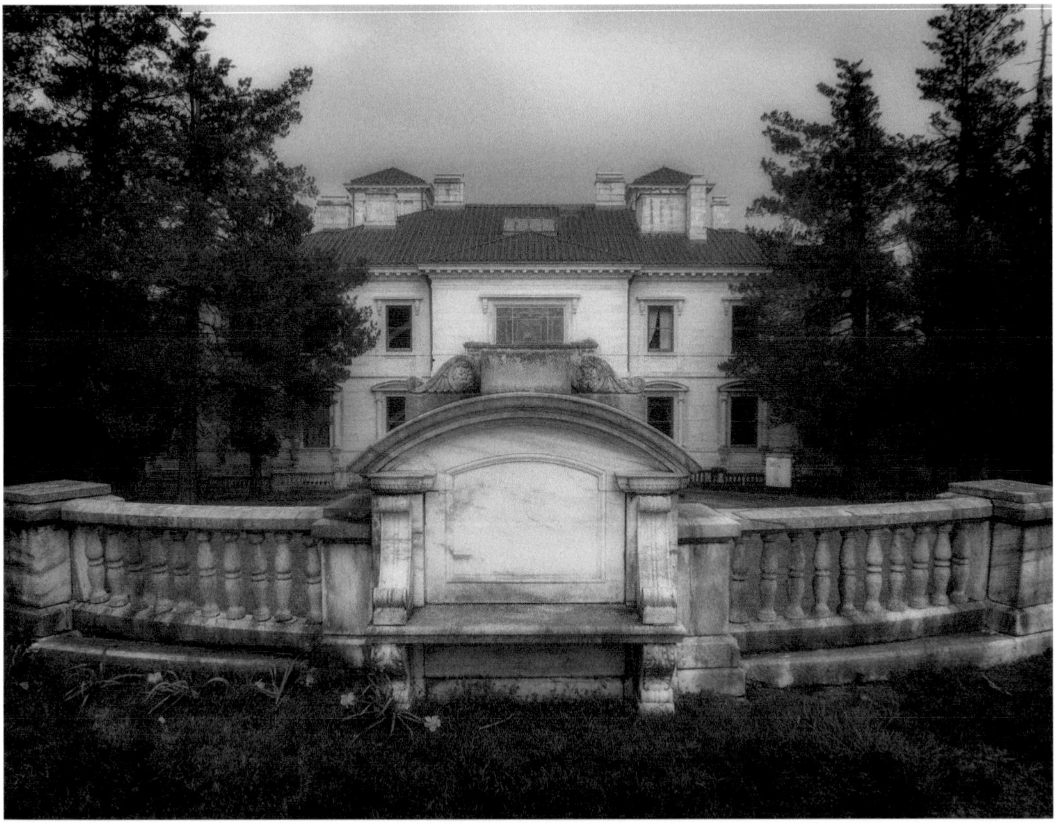

Right: Photo 115: THE WEATHERED STAIRS: It has been a while since we have looked at a stair photo. But seriously, these are different stairs, and I really liked this shot because of the way the light was illuminating the walkway at the bottom.

Below: Photo 116: TUNNEL VISION: This photo, and Photos 117–119, may look familiar to those who have been to the Italian Garden in Richmond's Maymont Park. There is a similar covered walkway in Maymont, although the one there is in much better condition. This photo is facing toward the Shenandoah Valley.

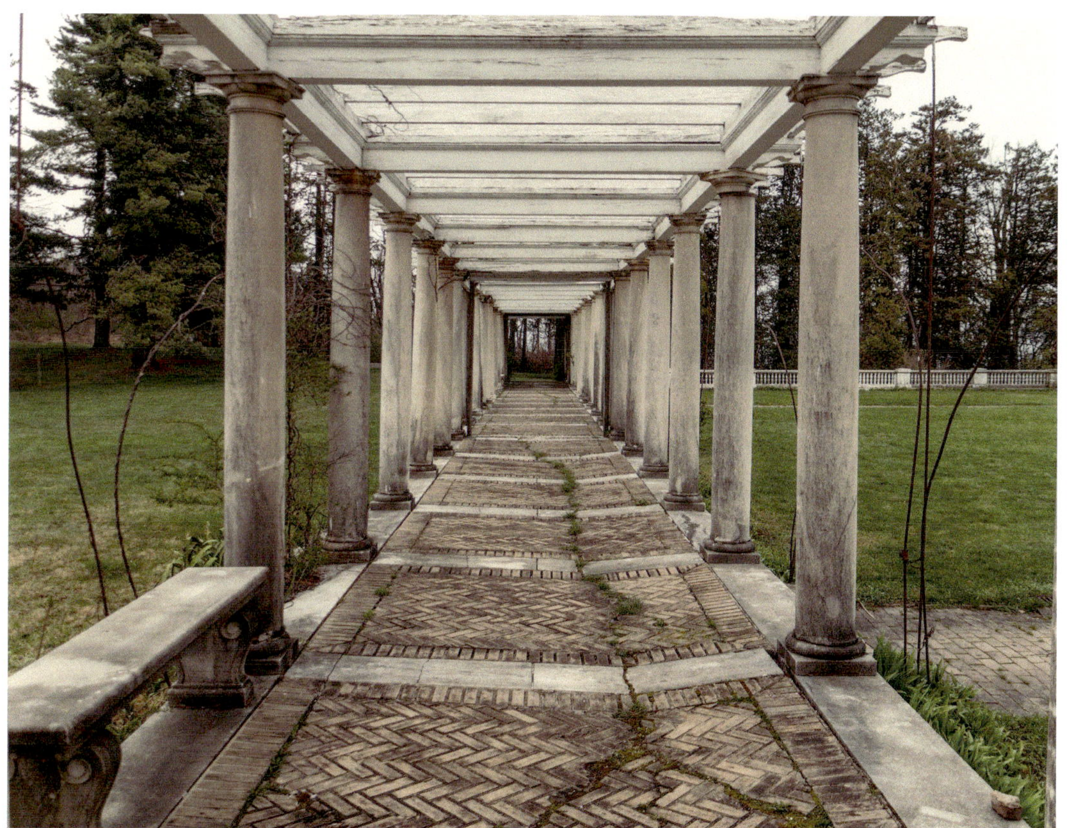

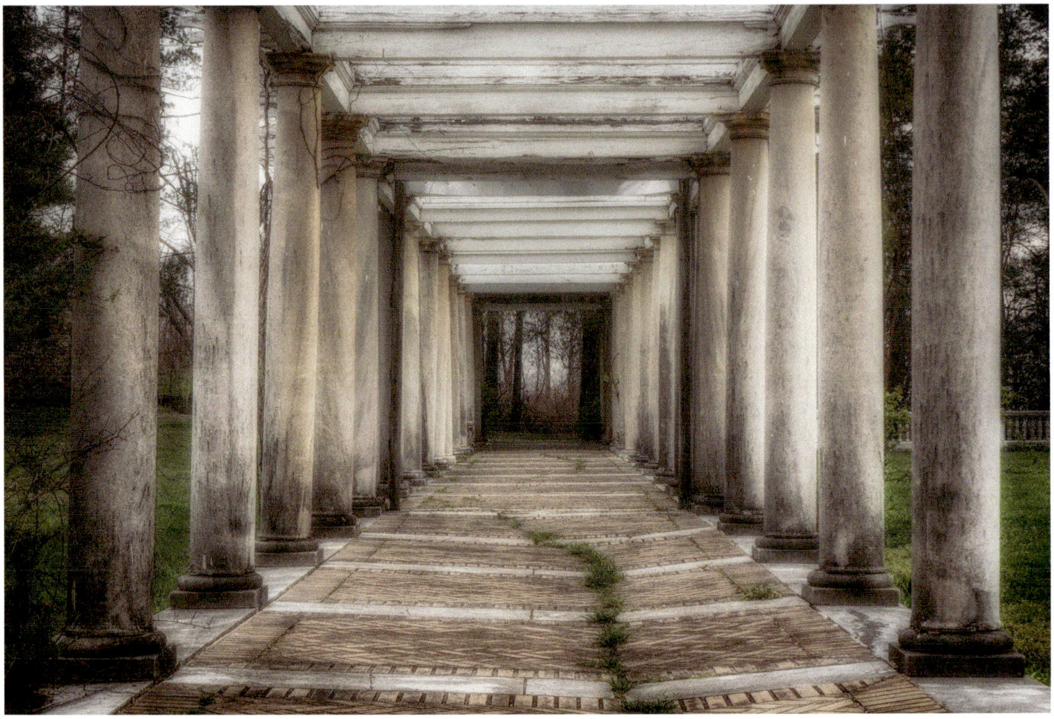

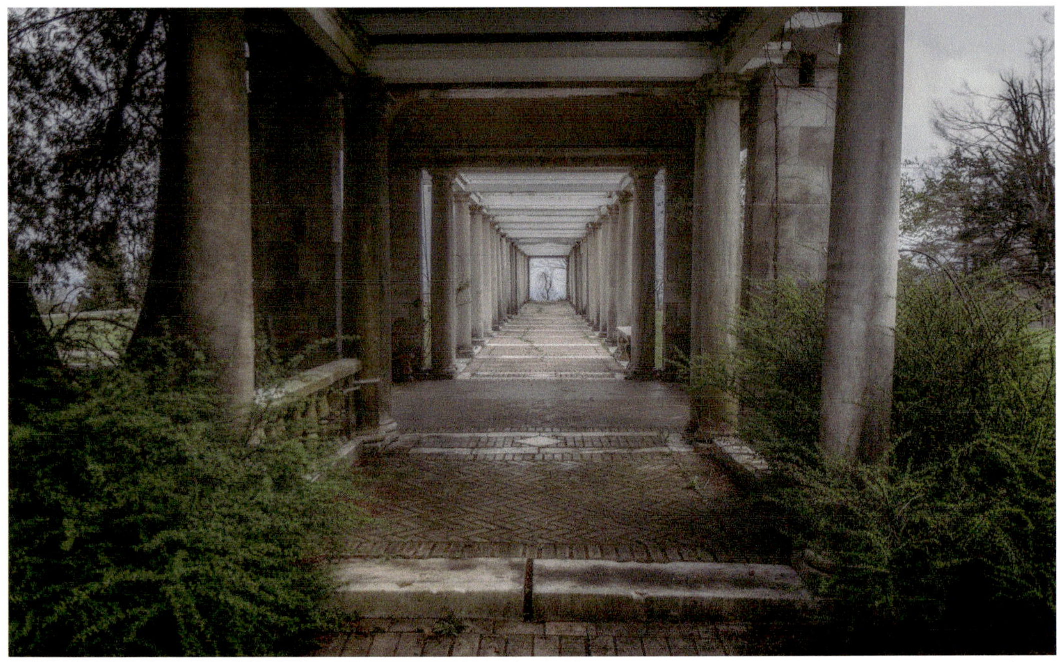

Photo 117: WALKWAY INTO THE WILD: This photo faces in the same direction as Photo 116 but is more zoomed in.

Photo 118: HISTORICAL PERSPECTIVE: This photo was taken at the opposite end of the walkway from where Photo 116 was taken and is facing toward the Rockfish Valley.

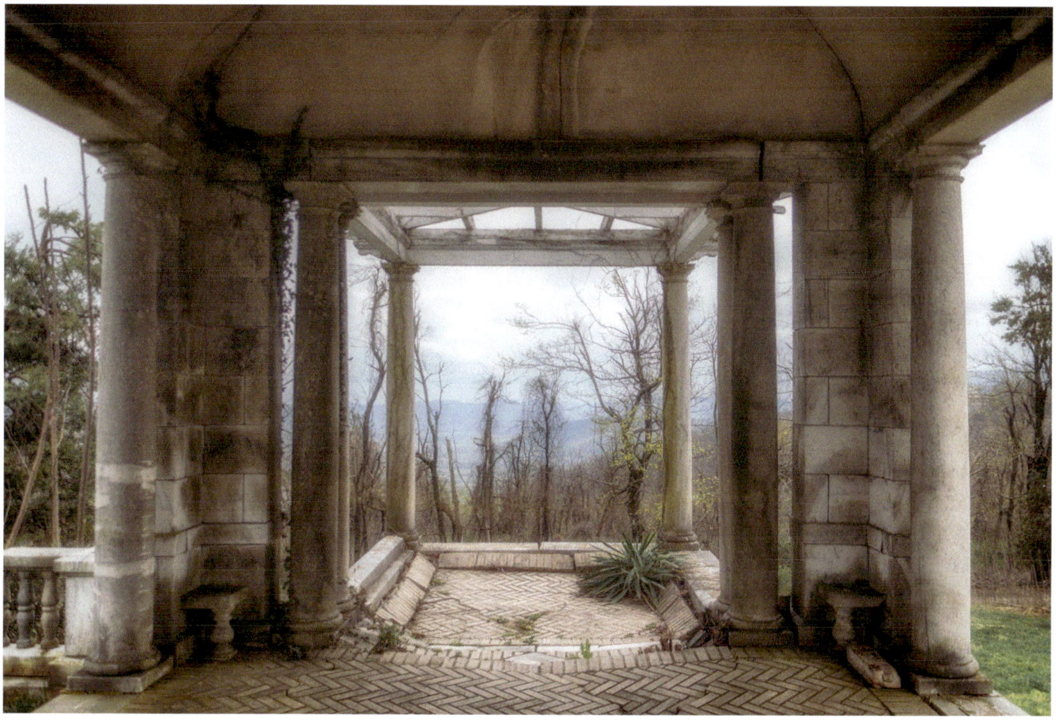

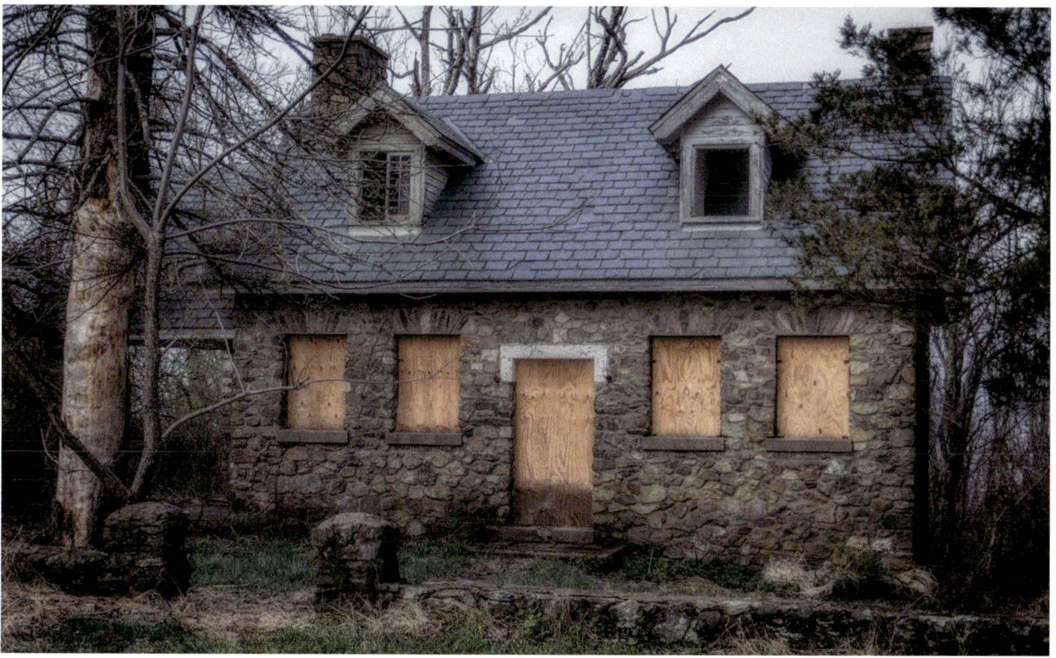

Photo 119: Mountainside Covered Walkway: This photo was taken at the same end of the walkway as was Photo 116, except facing in the opposite direction towards the Rockfish Valley.

Photo 120: The Golf House: At first glance, one might think that this little house was built as a guesthouse until one remembers that the mansion has thirty-six rooms. This little house was actually built during the days of the country club and was used for administrative purposes for the club.

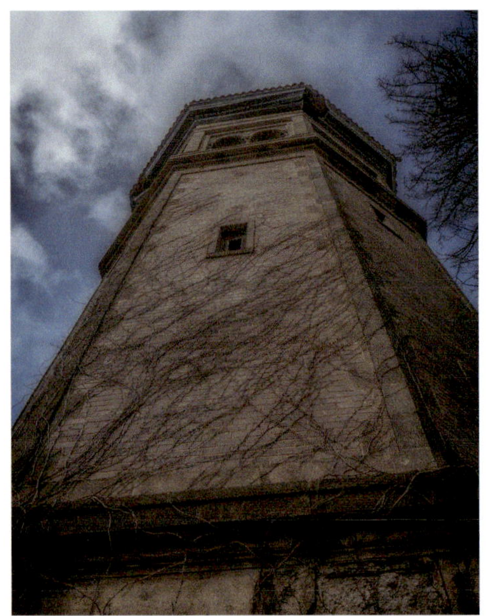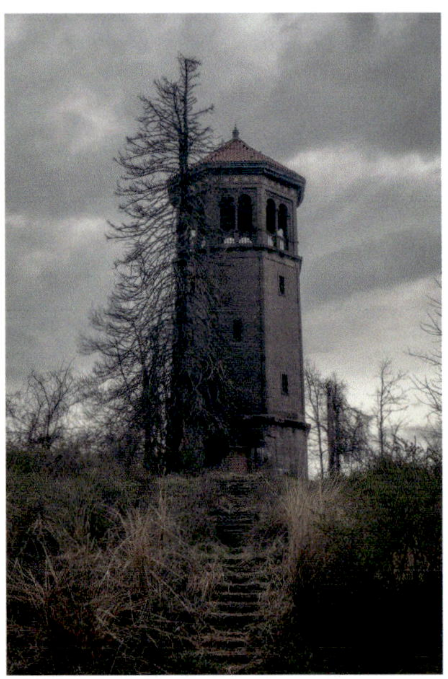

Above left: Photo 121: Towering Heights: This tower is one of the reasons the mansion was able to have running water. It was the water tower for the mansion. By the looks of it, I almost expect to see a princess letting down her long hair for a prince to use to scale to the top of the tower and rescue her from captivity.

Above right: Photo 122: The Dark Tower: This is the same tower as in Photo 121, except photographed from a distance. To me the weathered stairs in the foreground and the tall, leafless tree next to the tower add to the character of this shot. That tree, however, has been removed since this photo was taken.

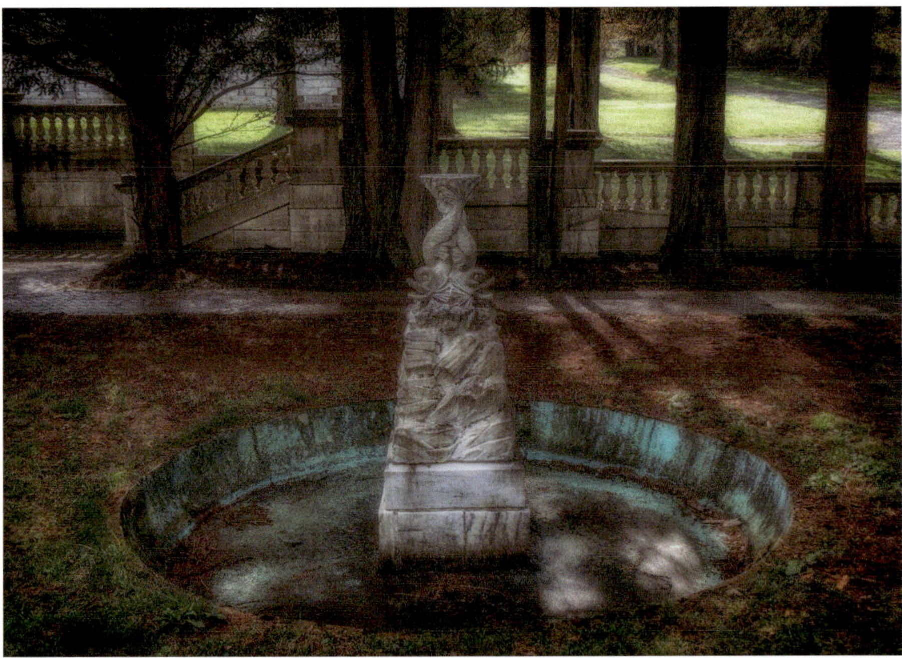

Photo 123: Empty Wishes: This is an old fountain on one end of the mansion. There is another one on the opposite end of the mansion as well.

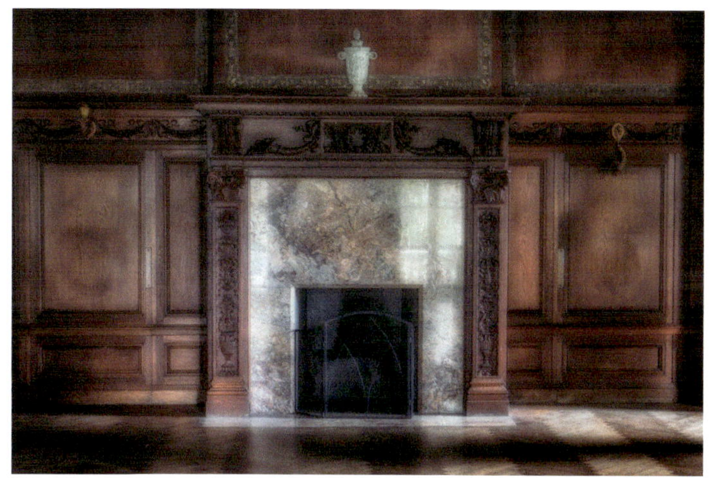 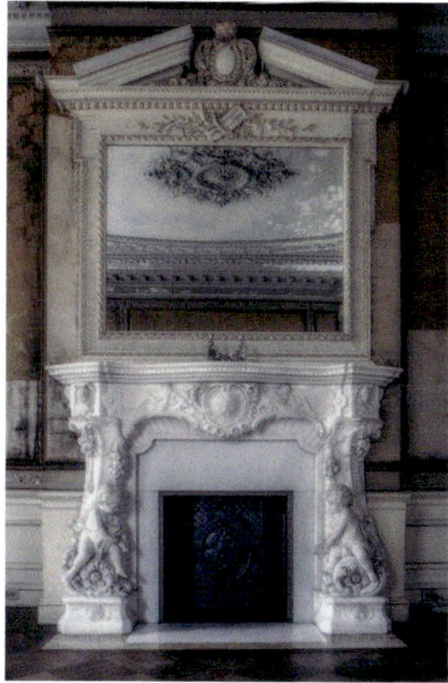

Above left: Photo 124: THE MASTERPIECE MANTLEPIECE: A beautiful fireplace in one of the rooms on the main floor with an incredibly detailed mantle.

Above right: Photo 125: THE SIDE PARLOR: Not to be outdone, this museum-quality mantle adorns a fireplace in another room on the main floor.

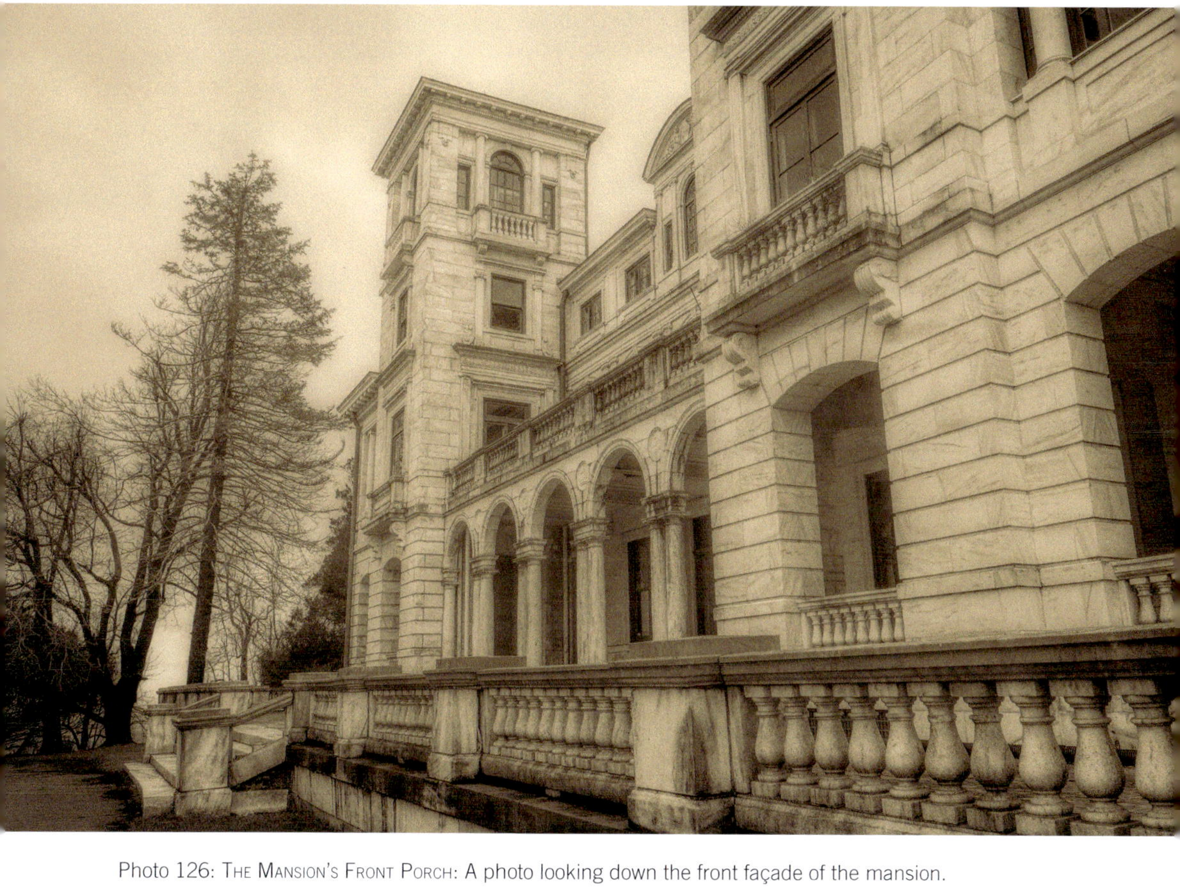

Photo 126: THE MANSION'S FRONT PORCH: A photo looking down the front façade of the mansion.

5

DUNNINGTON MANSION (POPLAR HILL)

Outside of the town of Farmville lies this next mansion. It is known as Dunnington Mansion (historically known as Poplar Hill) and is pictured in Photo 127.

Over the course of its history, Poplar Hill went through nine different owners, including the current owners. The original home on the property was built in 1748 as a four-room wooden farmhouse. Around 1830, a separate brick home was constructed and is still part of the mansion that stands today. Sometime between 1849 and 1860, two subsequent brick additions were added on to the house. By 1897, under the direction of then owners Walter Grey and India Dunnington, a massive expansion and renovation took place. During this expansion, four additional rooms were added to the house along with a conservatory, a tower (which contained two more small rooms), and the elegant front porch (which has now been removed for safety reasons).

There is currently a concerted effort being made to save the mansion. The non-profit organization spear-heading the effort is the Dunnington Mansion Foundation. Its president, Heather Beach, was gracious enough to supply me with a little more of the mansion's history:

Once a stately and beautiful Victorian manor, Poplar Hill has an extensive and rich history. Sadly, this is far from the truth today. Threatened by housing developments and woeful neglect, this amazing piece of architecture might soon be lost.

After being bought by developers in 2000 there were plans to make it the shining jewel of the future Manor Golf Course. Unfortunately, the money dried up for the developers and pieces of the property were sold to different investors. The golf course was constructed in 2004 and the mansion was ignored.

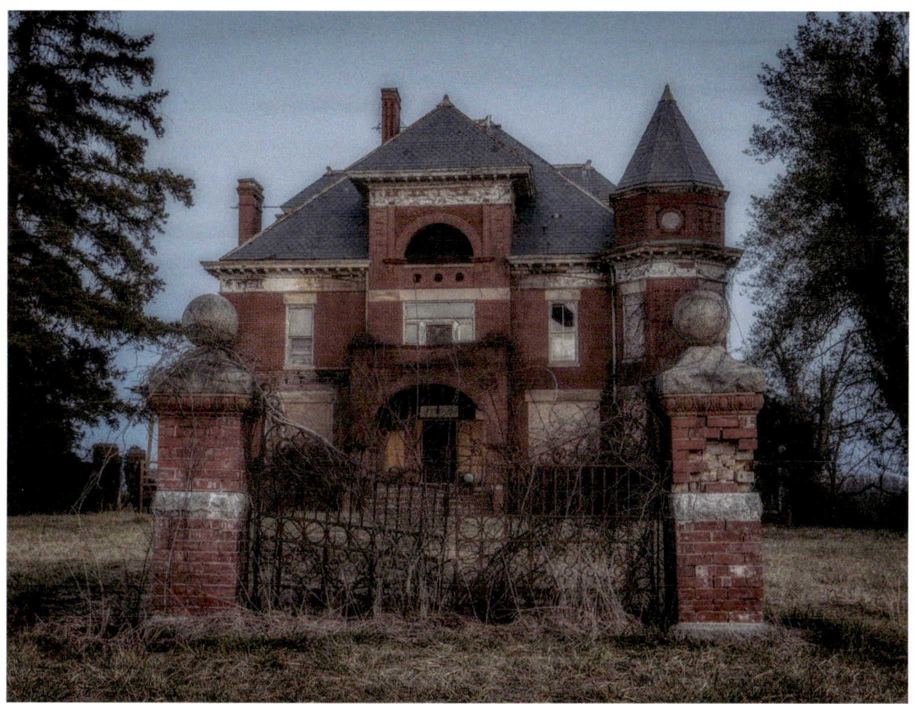

Photo 127: Dᴜɴɴɪɴɢᴛᴏɴ Mᴀɴsɪᴏɴ: The front façade of the Dunnington Mansion. The front porch canopy has since been meticulously disassembled for safety reasons until it can be safely rebuilt again. In the mansion's heyday, rows of hedges met up against each brick column of the front gate.

Over the last 23 years its former glory has slowly faded. Currently, the house is in various stages of decay and its future is seriously endangered. Exposed to the elements the beautiful plaster walls, once covered in opulent wallpaper, have started to crumble. Holes in the roof and broken windows have allowed decades of rain to pour into the interior. In some rooms entire ceilings have collapsed and the floors have fallen.

Broken and all but forgotten, its ghostly beauty is breathtaking. In silent defiance of its current state the mansion is still compelling and inspiring.

At the time of this writing, the foundation has been given two years to raise the necessary funds to purchase the mansion, otherwise it will be demolished to make way for development. More information about the mansion, including more of its history and info on ways that we can help to save it, can be found on the foundation's website: www.dunningtonmansion.org. Photos 128–158 were taken at the mansion.

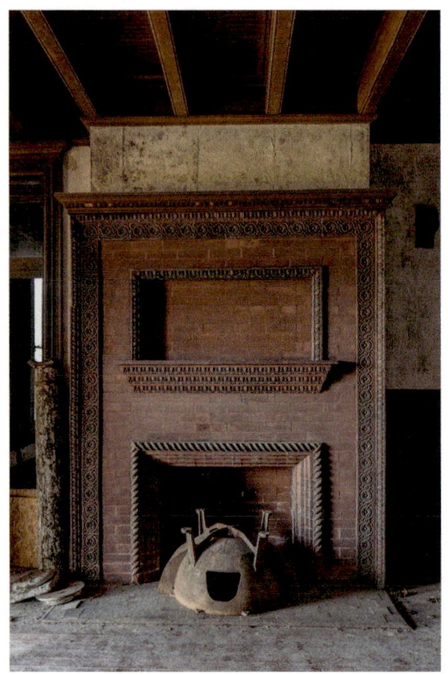 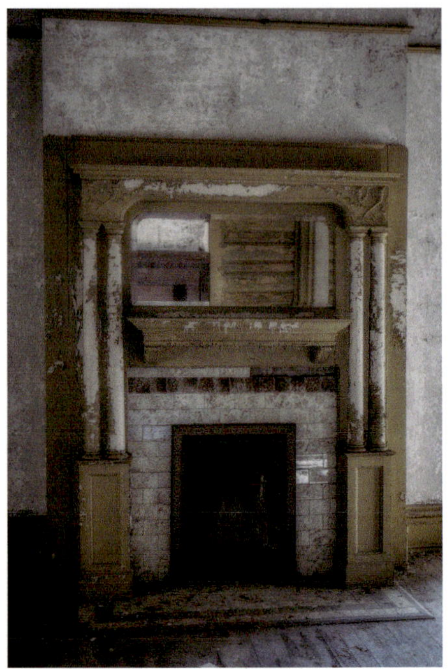

Above left: Photo 128: MASONIC EXCELLENCE: An old brick fireplace located near the front door of the mansion.

Above right: Photo 129: THE GOLDEN MANTLE: Another fireplace, this time located in one of the first floor living spaces.

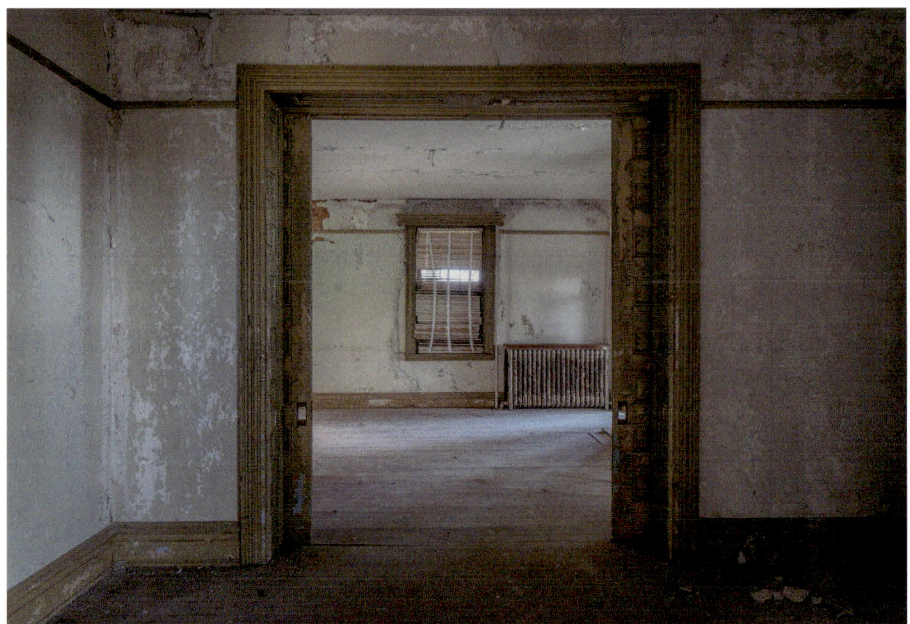

Photo 130: THE ADJOINING ROOM: The next room over from the one where the fireplace in Photo 129 is located. At one time, on Christmas Days of old, the large Christmas tree was located in the room through this doorway and these doors would be kept locked to prevent young ones from prematurely peeking at or opening their Christmas gifts.

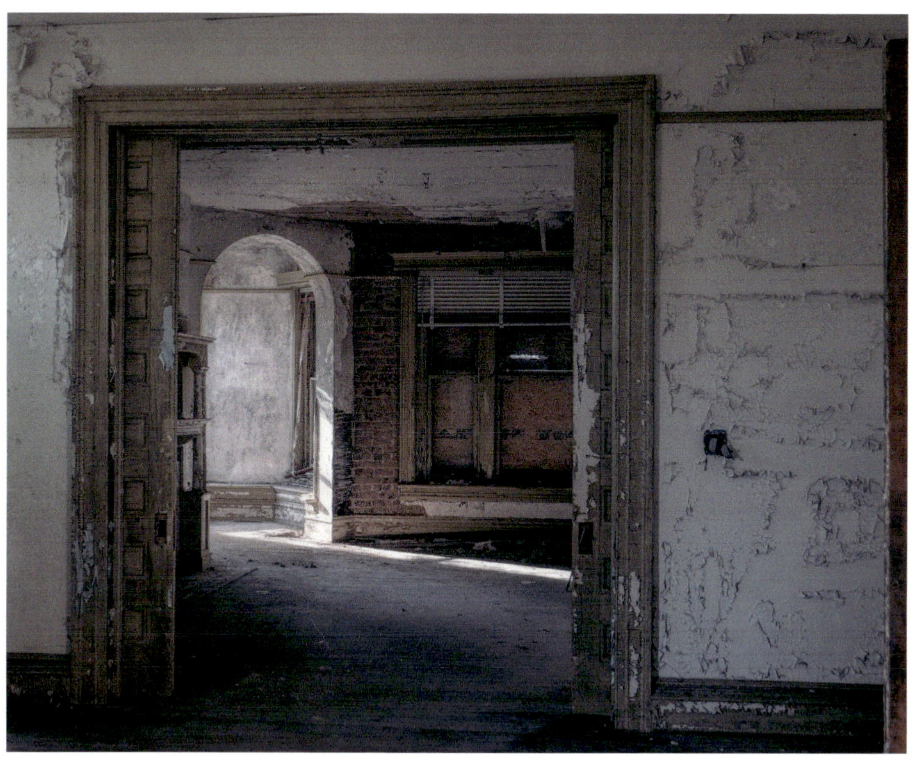

Photo 131: Into the Parlor: This shot is looking back in the other direction through the doors in photo 130.

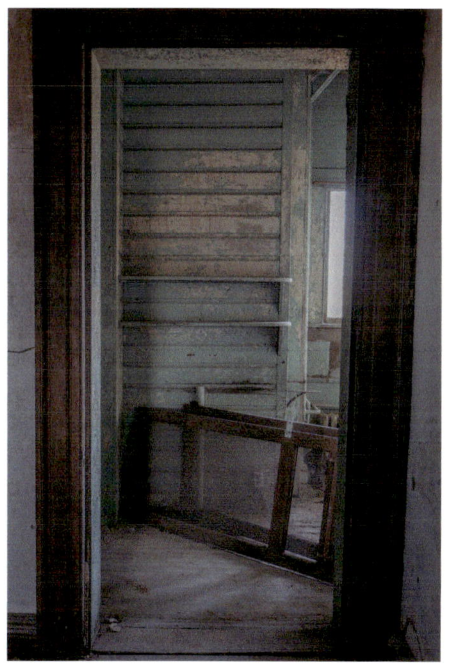

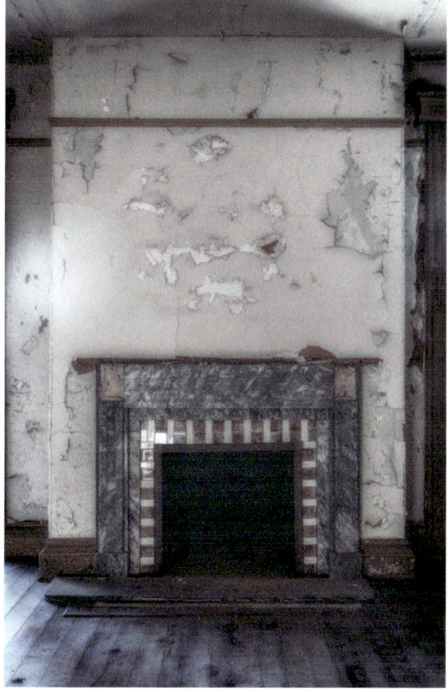

Above left: Photo 132: The Aqua Room: A view through a doorway looking into a back room.

Above right: Photo 133: Checkered History: A fireplace located in the room where Photo 131 was taken.

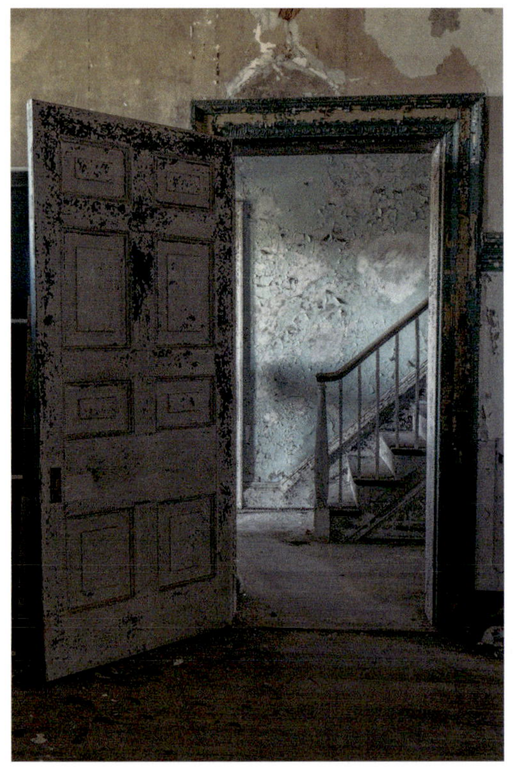

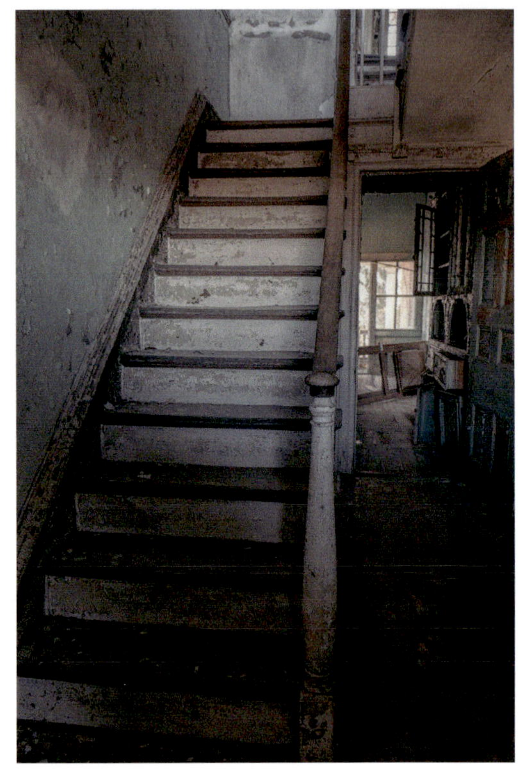

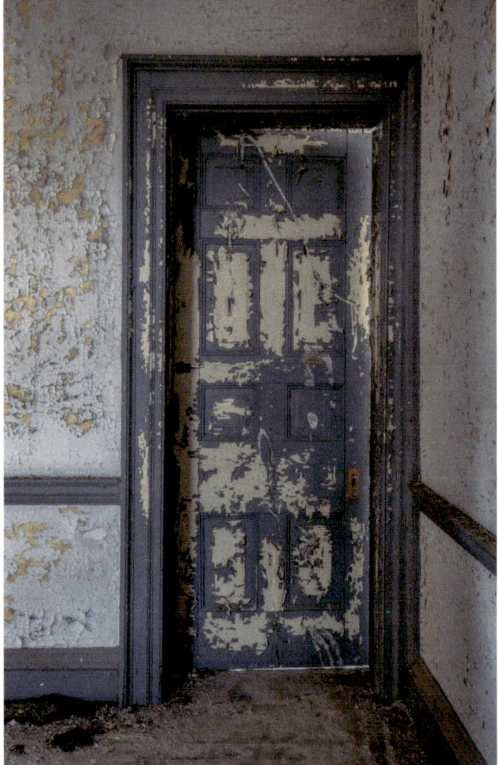

Above left: Photo 134: Door to the Back Stairs: The view from a downstairs room looking through a doorway to the hall where the back stairs are located.

Above right: Photo 135: The Back Stairs: In case you were not able to guess from my incredibly creative title, this photo is a shot of the back staircase in the mansion.

Left: Photo 136: The Battered Doorway: Through the years as I have viewed and admired abandonment photography from many different photographers, I always seem to be the most intrigued by those photos that feature paint that has slowly chipped away over time.

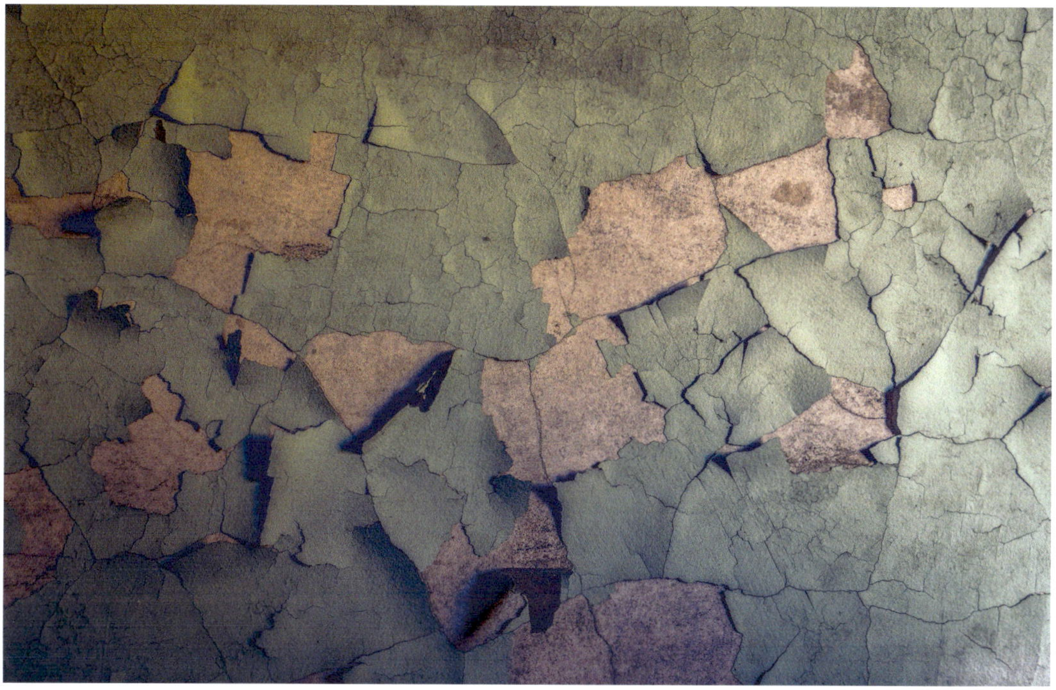

Photo 137: Puzzle Pieces: This shot resembled an incomplete jigsaw puzzle to me. In fact, I wonder if this shot might actually make a good jigsaw puzzle!

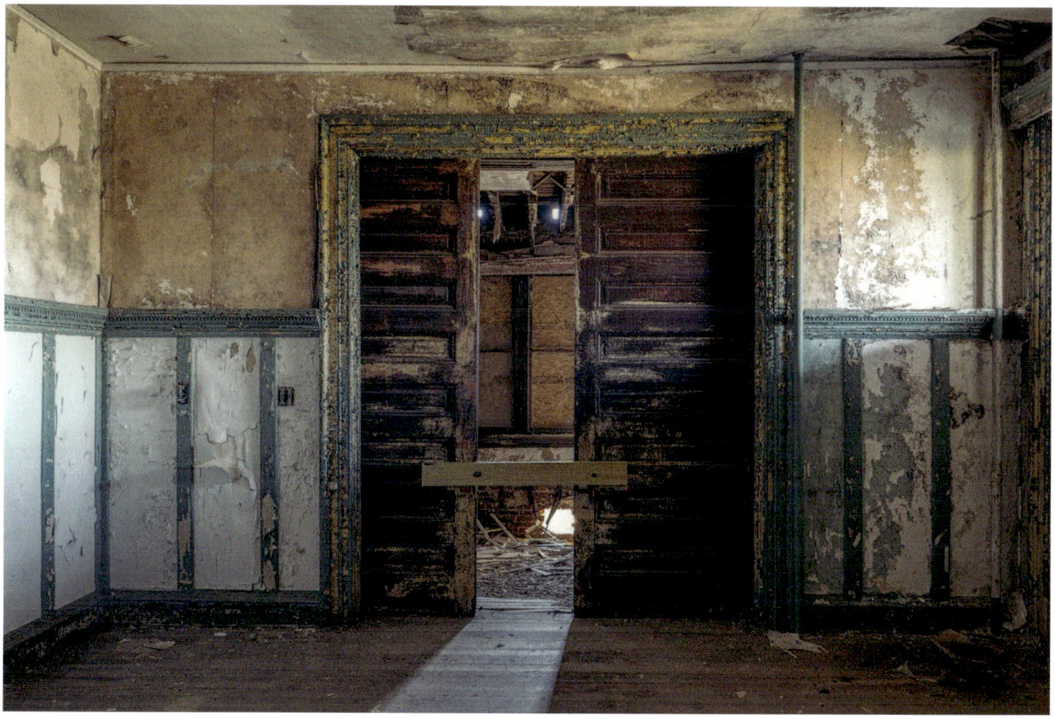

Photo 138: Do Not Enter: Seriously, do not enter. This doorway has been boarded closed due to the roof having partially caved-in in the adjacent room.

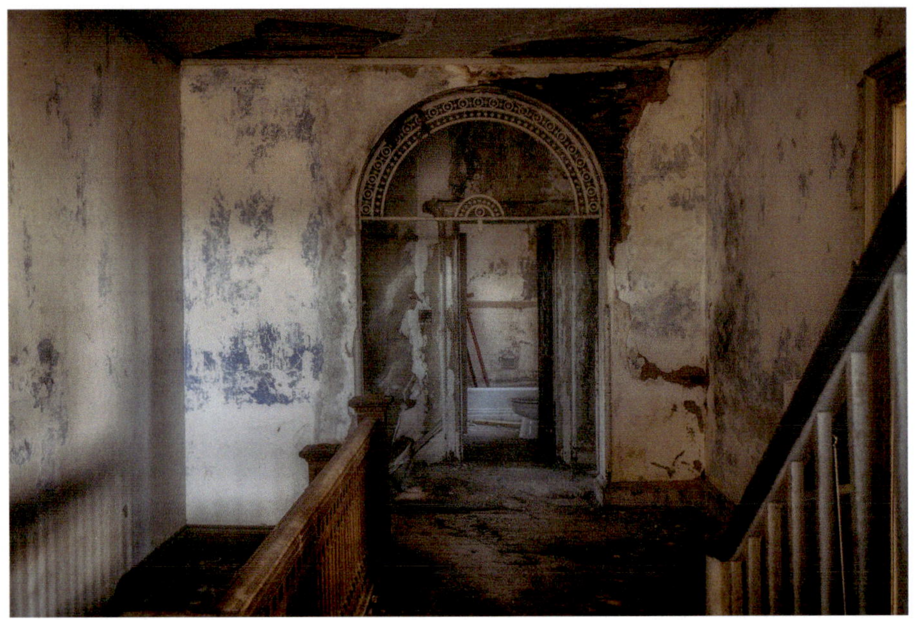

Photo 139: Second-Floor Landing: The landing on the second floor as you come up the front set of stairs (on the left). The stairs on the right lead up to the third floor but they were not accessible to us for safety reasons.

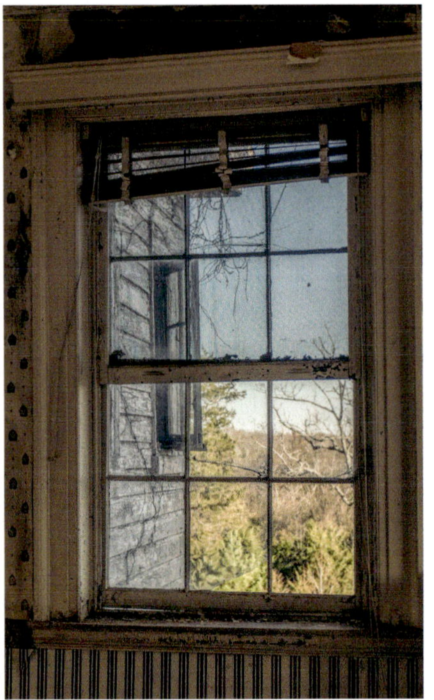

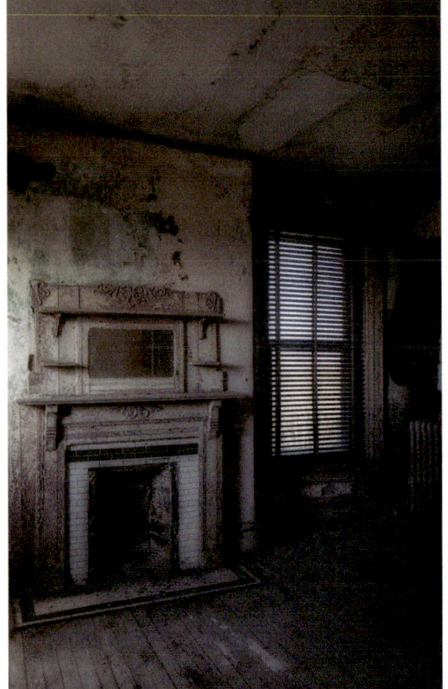

Above left: Photo 140: Back Window: A view through one of the second-floor windows at the back of the mansion.

Above right: Photo 141: The Forgotten Guest Room: One of the second-floor bedrooms.

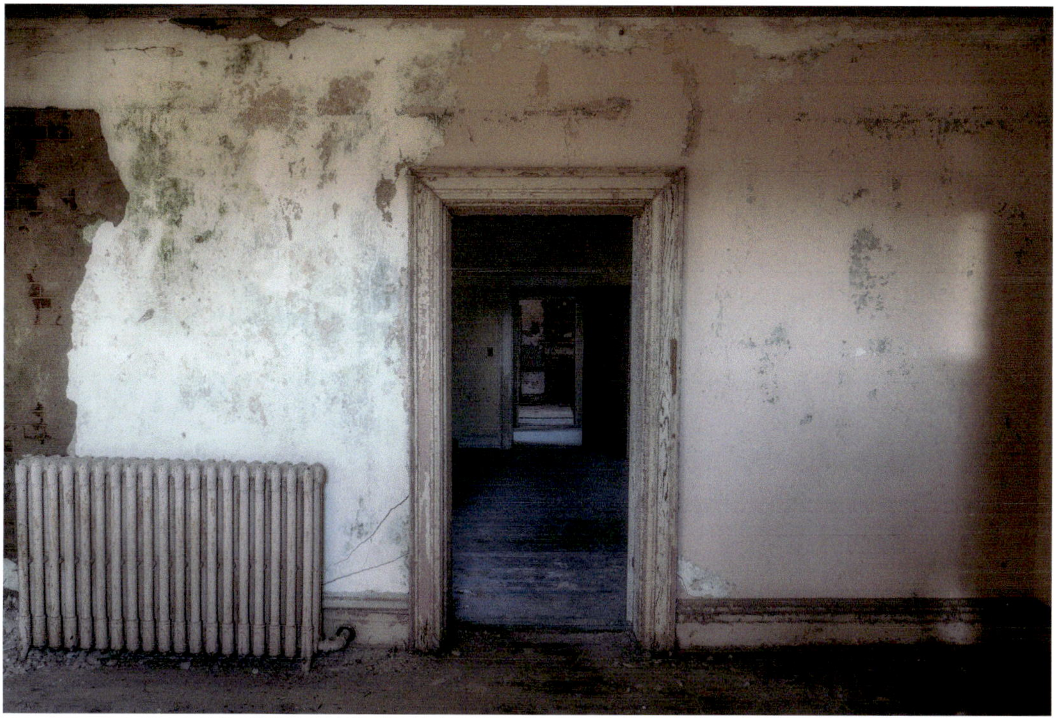

Photo 142: DOORWAYS OF YESTERYEAR: A view through aligned doorways in adjacent second-floor bedrooms.

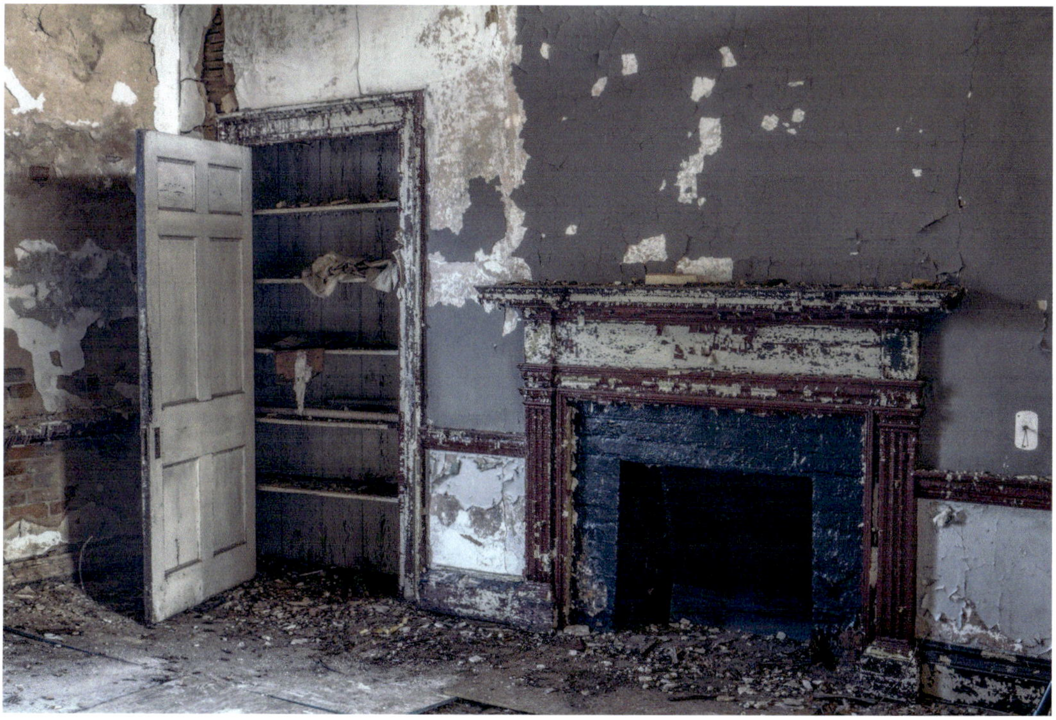

Photo 143: THE WEATHERED RED MANTLE: A fireplace that has long since seen better days in one of the rooms on the second floor.

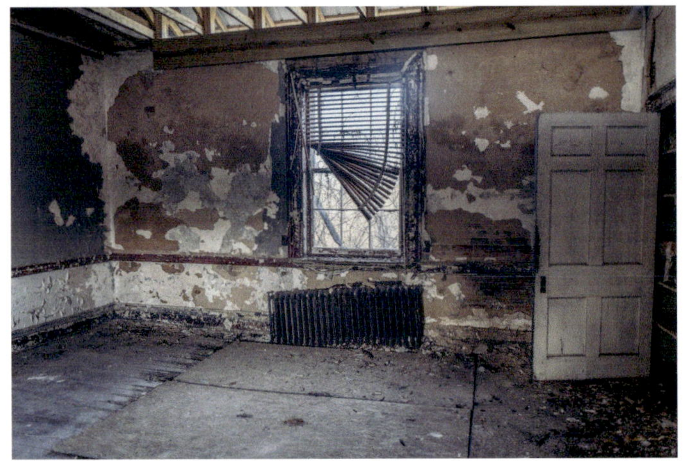

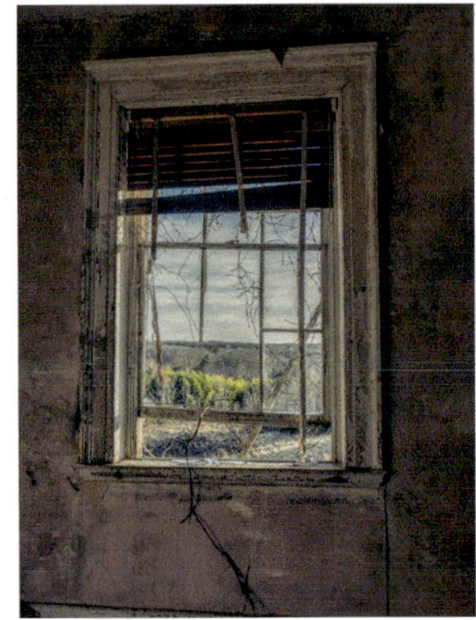

Above left: Photo 144: DRAW THE BLINDS: One of the rooms at the back of the mansion on the second floor. You can see some of the reinforcement that has taken place at the top of the photo.

Above right: Photo 145: WINDOW OF TIME: A view from another second-floor window.

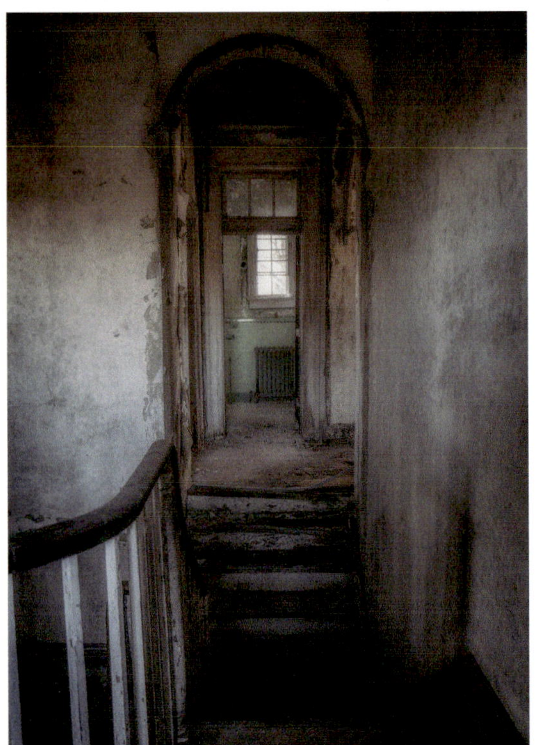

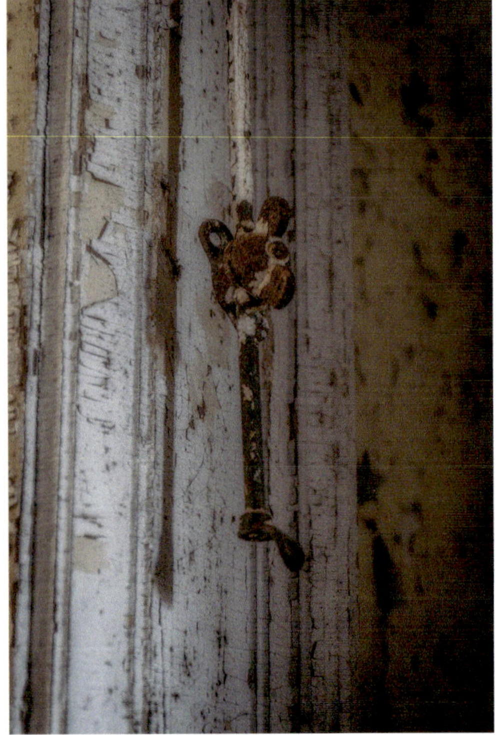

Above left: Photo 146: INTO THE CORRIDOR: A look down a second-floor corridor where the back staircase converges with two other short sets of stairs.

Above right: Photo 147: HANGING RELIC: I am not exactly sure what this is, but it was hanging from a door as though it was asking to be the subject of one of the many photographers' photos, so I obliged.

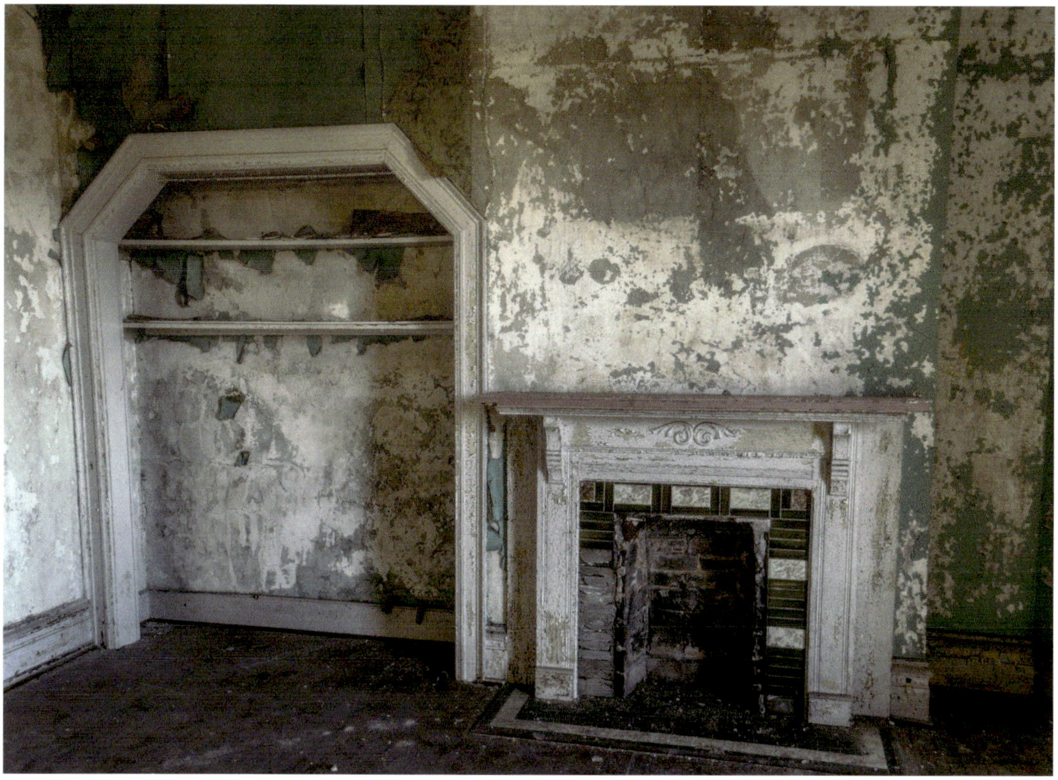

Above: Photo 148: THE GREEN ROOM: Another bedroom on the second floor. I had to wait a couple of hours before taking this photo because prior to that point, the sun was shining through a window, causing a giant glare on the wall above the fireplace.

Right: Photo 149: VIEW FROM THE SIDE WINDOW: A view from one of the second-floor windows overlooking the solarium.

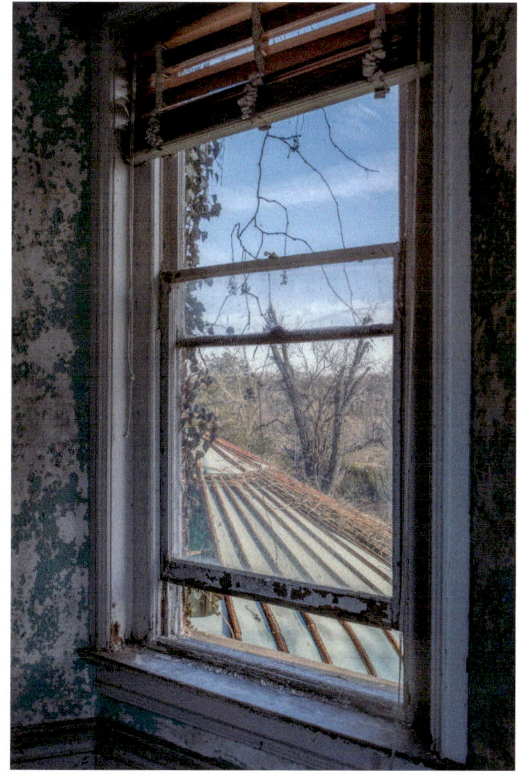

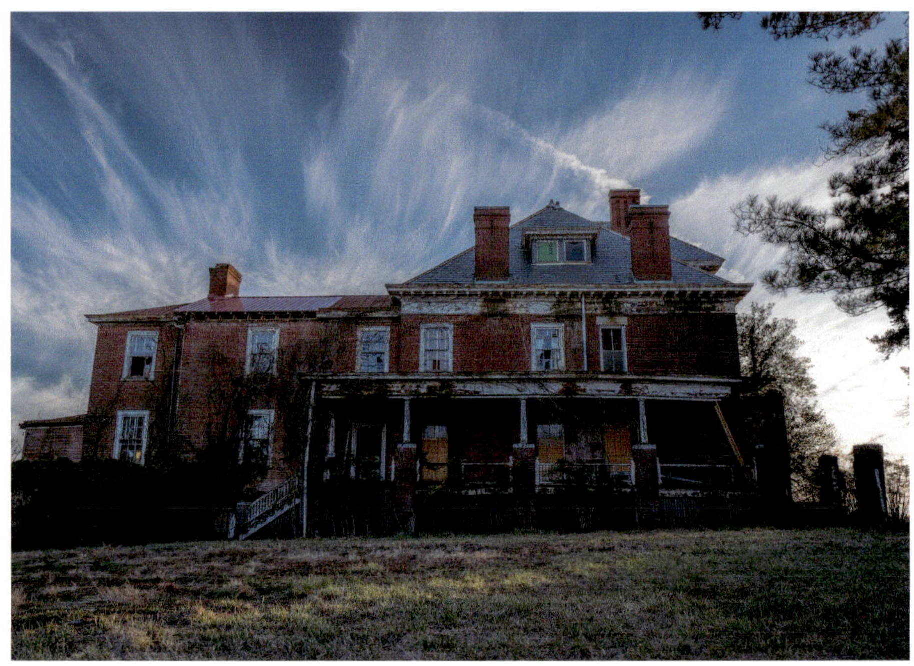

Photo 150: East Side of the Mansion: In all honesty this is actually the north side of the mansion but since the sun was setting somewhere on the other side of the mansion, I named this photo the east side. To me, this lawn looks like a perfect location for a spring or autumn picnic.

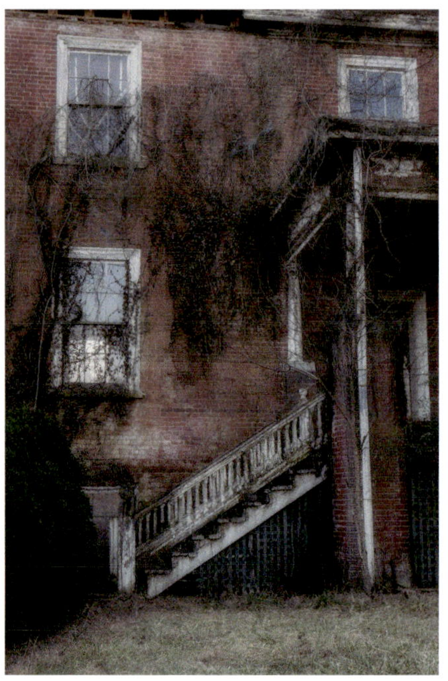

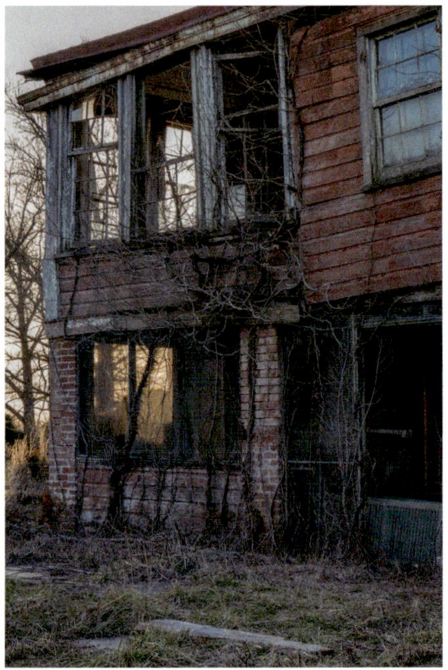

Above left: Photo 151: The Back Porch Stairs: A closer view of the stairs on the porch shown in Photo 150.

Above right: Photo 152: Back of the Old Mansion: A shot of the back part of the mansion with the light of the setting sun shining through some of the windows.

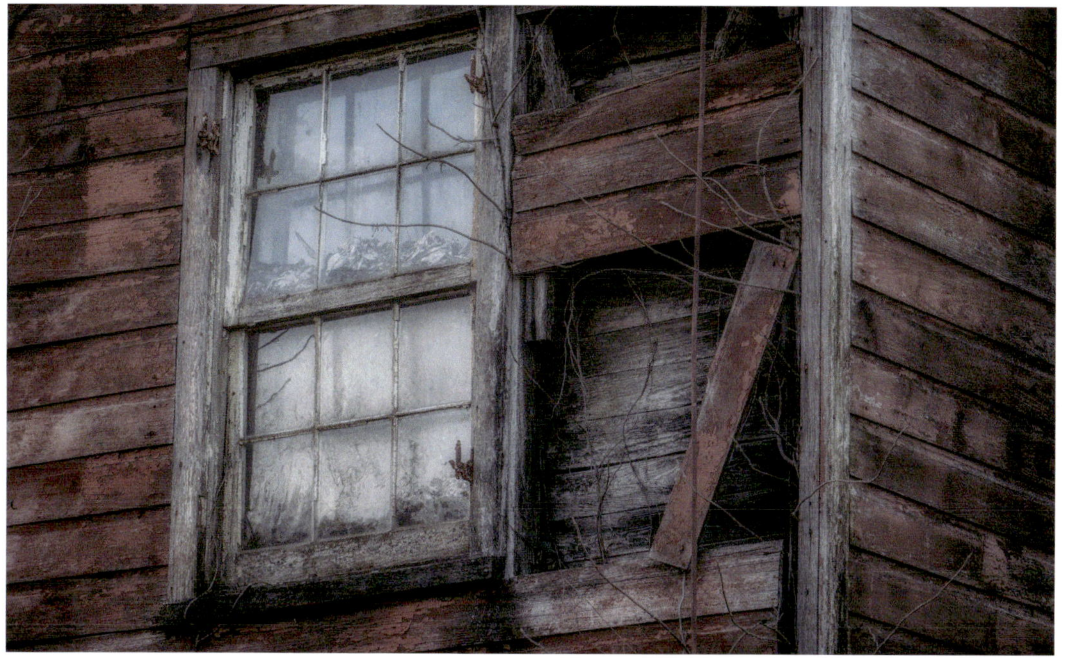

Photo 153: WINDOW OF OPPORTUNITY: In an amazing turn of events, here is a photo of a window taken from the outside! I really like how the missing pieces of siding make it look as though there once was a second window next to this one.

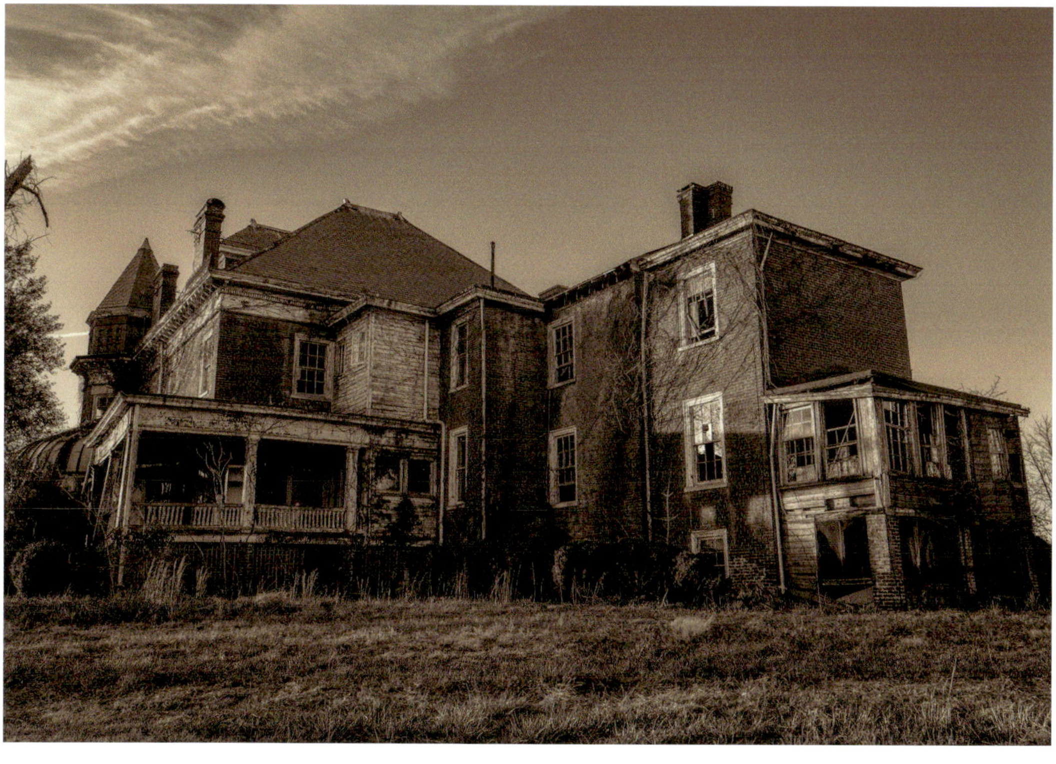

Photo 154: THE MANSION BACKYARD: A shot taken from behind the mansion that I thought looked best in sepia.

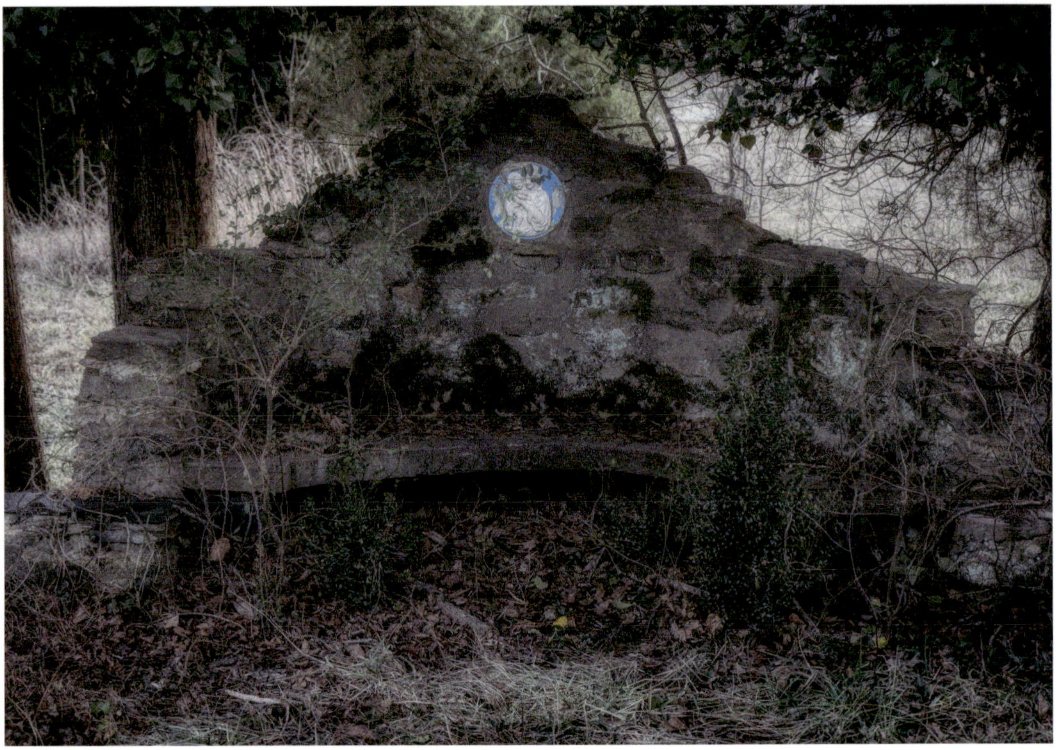

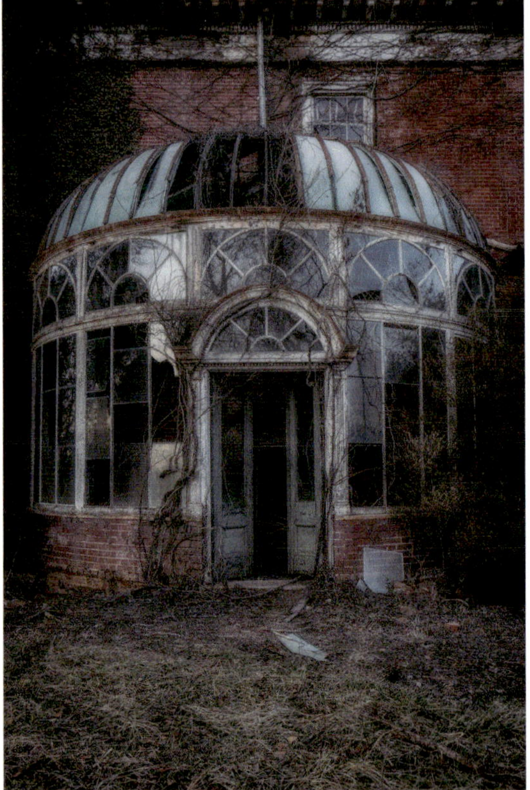

Above: Photo 155: SMALL CAPS BENCHED: A nearby bench with an engraving depicting the Virgin Mary holding the baby Christ Child.

Left: Photo 156: SOLARIUM SILENCE: A close-up shot of the solarium where the owners of the mansion used to grow their own seasonal flowers that were used for arrangements throughout the mansion.

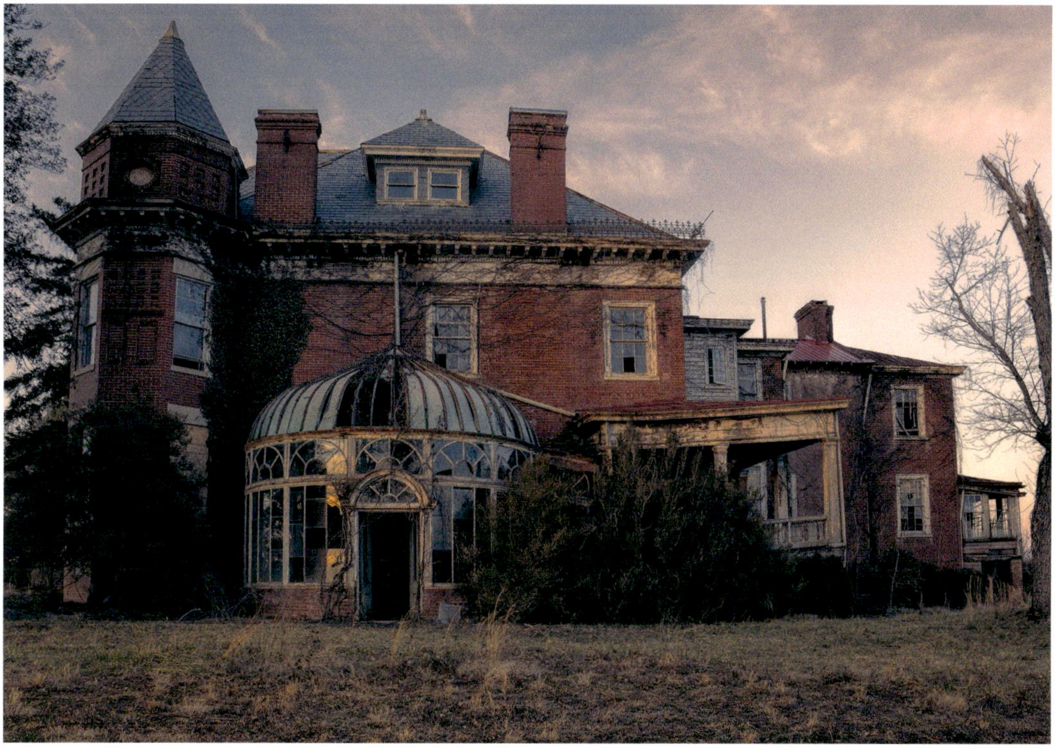

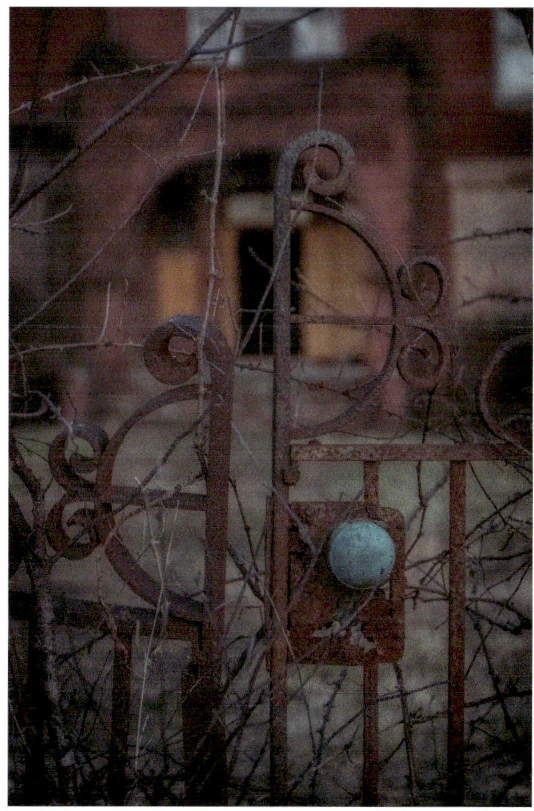

Above: Photo 157: ABANDONED DUSK: A shot of the south facing side of the mansion taken as the sun was setting behind me and off to the left.

Right: Photo 158: THE FRONT GATE: A close-up view of the front gate showcasing the beautiful teal color of the knob as a result of years of decay. I thought it fitting to use this photo as my final photo of the mansion to signify the closing of the door of this chapter as well as the upcoming conclusion of this book.

6

IN CLOSING

I began this book by writing about the quickness with which time passes and how quickly decay can set in. We have just looked at 158 photos detailing decay in various forms. For those affiliated with the buildings and automobiles in those photos, if they are still with us today, I am sure they would say that it feels just like yesterday that those objects were new and being used daily. If my grandfather were still with us, I am sure he would say the same about these last two images. Back in the 1980s, he drove a propane truck and delivered to homes all around the Richmond area. As kids we used to get so excited during the summers to see his big propane truck backing into our driveway so he could grab a cold glass of water. The home in Photo 159 is located close to my own home. My grandfather used to tell me that he used to deliver propane to that house. Now it sits empty, adjacent to multiple modern subdivisions as a reminder of when this area was once considered to be rural.

Photo 160 also relates to my grandfather as this forgotten road was once part of his propane delivery route. It is now hidden by trees and unknown to passersby even though it only lies several yards from the main road that now runs through the area. It is a reminder of how quickly deterioration can take place with the absence of care and maintenance. If there is anything I would like you to take with you by reading this book, it would be to not allow relationships with loved ones to become like this old road. Time moves quicker than we think. Those who are now in our lives may disappear from them very rapidly and when that happens it is far better to be able to look back and not have to regret words left unsaid, actions not taken or visits unfulfilled. And if you happen to be driving down an old country road one day and come across an old derelict building or home, try to see the beauty in it, for beauty can exist anywhere if we choose to see it. That is my wish.

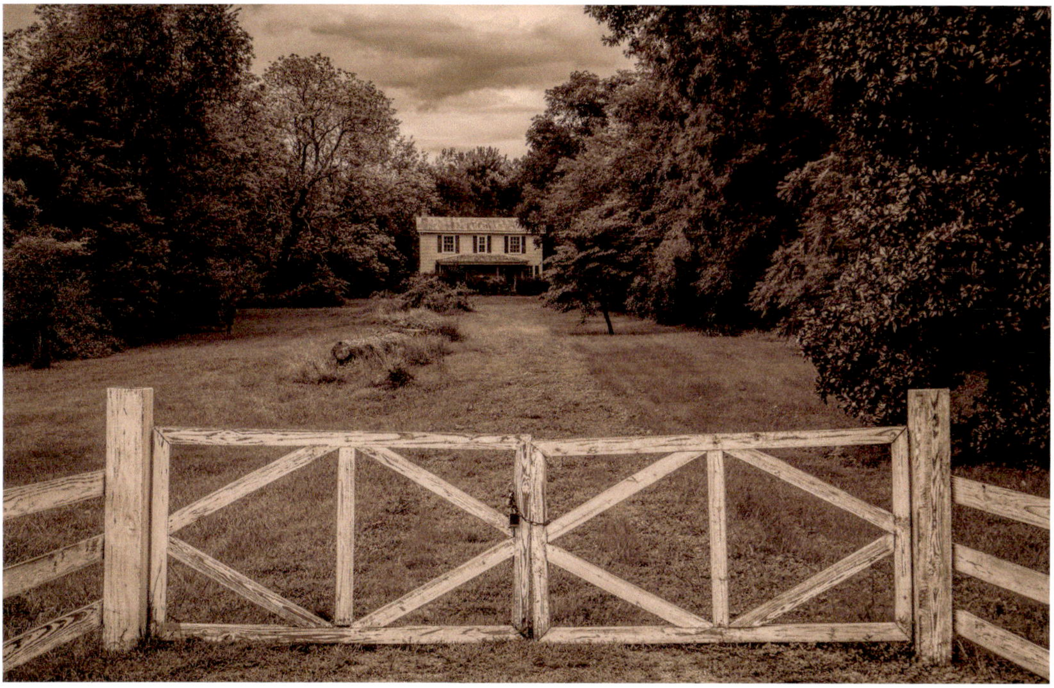

Photo 159: IMPENDING DEMISE: I titled this photo that way because at the time plans had been presented to the county to demolish this old house and build a subdivision behind it. Those plans did not come to fruition and as of this writing this old beauty still stands.

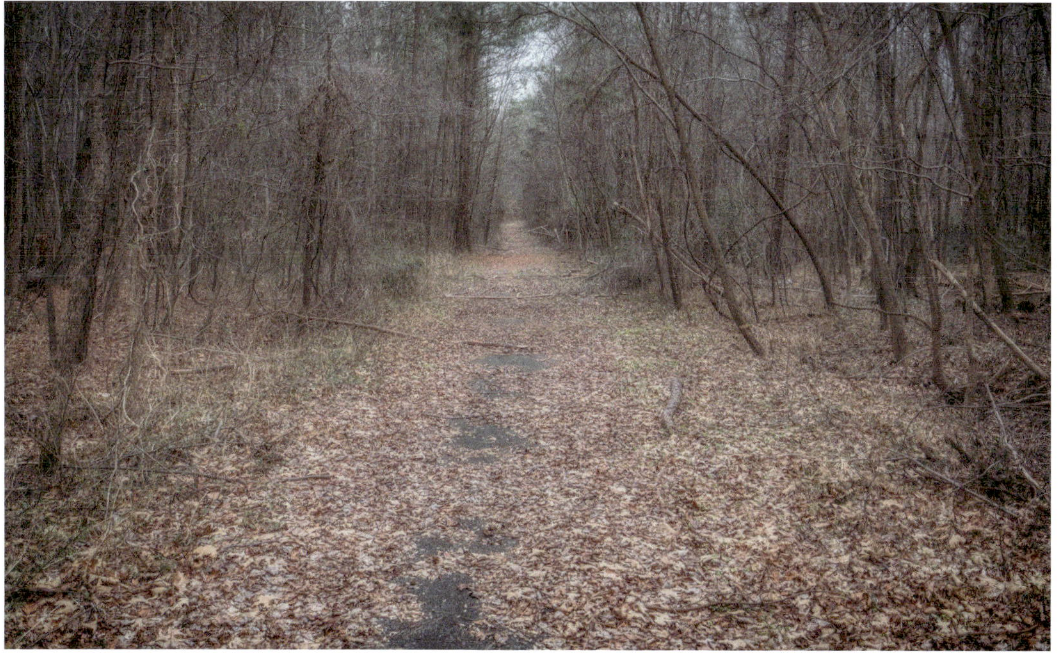

Photo 160: THE LONE AND DREARY ROAD: What is left of an old road that my late grandfather used to travel while delivering propane in the 1980s. Now it lies unused as the surrounding trees, as well as impending development, converge upon it. In fact, as of this writing, trees are already being cleared in this area for more development.

ABOUT THE AUTHOR

Sean Toler is an amateur photographer living in the Richmond, Virginia, area. He enjoys photographing majestic landscapes, especially at dawn and dusk. He also loves to capture images of decay and abandonment when he is able. If you would like to see more of his work, visit his Linktree page at: linktr.ee/seantolerphoto.